**What Price Fame?**

What Price Fame?

TYLER COWEN

Harvard University Press

Cambridge, Massachusetts

London, England

2000

Library of Congress Cataloging-in-Publication Data

Cowen, Tyler.
  What price fame? / Tyler Cowen.
      p. cm.
  Includes bibliographical references and index.
  ISBN 0-674-00155-9
  1. Fame. I. Title.
BJ1470.5.C69 1999
306.4—dc21   99-045903

Contents

Every man, however hopeless his pretensions may appear, has some project by which he hopes to rise to reputation; some art by which he imagines that the attention of the world will be attracted; some quality, good or bad, which discriminates him from the common herd of mortals, and by which others may be persuaded to love, or compelled to fear him.

—Samuel Johnson, *The Rambler*, 1751

1 The Intensity of Fame in Modern Society

Some people desire praise for the mere sake of recognition: Katharine Hepburn once remarked, "When I started out I didn't have any desire to be an actress or to learn how to act. I just wanted to be famous."[1]

Isaac Newton sought acclaim for his achievements in science. He engaged in long and costly battles with Robert Hooke over priority in optics and celestial mechanics, and with Gottfried Wilhelm Leibniz over the discovery of the differential calculus. Newton expected no money for establishing his originality but he did want recognition of his excellence. He wrote twelve versions of his claim to priority in discovering the calculus and appointed a committee—packed with his supporters—to adjudicate the case.[2]

Other people pursue fame as a means to get money or power or sex, or out of a complex combination of motives. Princess Diana courted the press to have a public counterweight to the royal family, which she perceived as allied against her. The altruistic, such as Mother Teresa, seek fame to help others through preaching or fund-raising.

For many artists fame complements the value of creative self-expression. Ludwig van Beethoven loved composing music, but he probably would have enjoyed it less if no one ever listened to the product. Many athletes play for the thrill of winning the game, but their enjoyment of the competition feeds on the cheers of the crowd and the sense of achieving a place in sport history. Marcel Proust shut out visitors from his cork-lined room, where he wrote, but he probably expected to be immortalized in the literary canon. Even the most introverted drives and motives are set in a social context and amplified by the potential for achieving fame.[3]

Mark David Chapman, the assassin of John Lennon, told Barbara Walters that "I thought by killing him I would acquire his fame." John Hinckley fired at Ronald Reagan to gain the attention of Jodie Foster. Arthur Bremer shot George Wallace in a quest for recognition, while worrying that his target was not famous enough to guarantee his immortality. Seeking infamy is part pathology, part laziness and lack of talent. For individuals with no moral scruples, infamy can prove the easiest or sometimes only way of getting attention.[4]

Quests for fame influence culture, business, politics, and everyday life. Adam Smith viewed the search for approval as "the end of half the labours of human life." David Hume, in his *Enquiry Concerning Human Understanding,* wrote of the "love of fame; which rules, with such uncontrolled authority, in all generous minds, and is often the grand object of all their designs and undertakings."[5]

Fame influences the behavior of fans no less powerfully. Many individuals enjoy praising and expressing enthusiasm for its own sake. They love to cheer, clap, visit monuments, make pilgrimages, give homage, or create laudatory artworks. In essence, fans are consumers, but they are consumers of a special sort. Fans are consumers who pay, at least in part, with praise.

The teenagers behind Beatlemania enjoyed screaming together, storming barricades together, and fainting together. Loving the Beatles *with other people* was more fun than loving them in solitude. Dedicated football fans gather before games and hold cookouts, drink beer, talk sports, hug each other, and catch up on personal news and gossip. Before a game, an NFL stadium parking lot radiates an air of intense bonding and sharing. Fans drive hundreds of miles to partake in these pregame gatherings, which are often a bigger attraction than the game itself. One Green Bay Packer fan said about pregame meetings: "This is all I want in life. It's all I love." The fame of celebrities creates a collective space in which fans share their emotional and aesthetic aspirations.[6]

Some fans are voyeurs at heart. The web site of Jennifer Ringley, an otherwise "ordinary" person, receives 500,000 hits daily. The site consists of scenes from Jennifer's daily life—reading, sleeping, and talking to friends (her sex life is not shown).[7]

Fans use stars as a way of advertising their tastes, distinguishing themselves from others, signaling their cultural standing, and seeking out the like-minded. Fans follow the same performers as their friends, if only to argue about them or to share their favorite moments from a movie or television program. Strangers and business associates use professional sports and celebrities as a comfortable topic of conversation, just as they use the weather. Fans attend conventions to make friends with the like-minded or to look for romance.[8]

Celebrities serve as a medium for political discussion and "education." Marlon Brando's support for Indian rights, the opposition of Muhammad Ali (then Cassius Clay) to the Vietnam War, and Jane Fonda's campaign against nuclear power are known to almost everyone, and have swayed many people. A 1981 study looked at how well Americans knew the political views of six stars: John Wayne, Robert Redford, Joan Baez, Jane Fonda, Dick Gregory, and Marlon Brando. The *lowest* public score was for Robert Redford: "only" 94 percent of the American public could associate him with the political issues he advocated; John Wayne's figure was 99 percent. Most of these same fans cannot name their representatives in Congress, much less identify their positions. The same study indicated that 80 percent of Americans had discussed the political views of celebrities with their friends. More than half of the 500 adults surveyed said they regarded celebrities as a fair and reliable source of information about public issues. One third admitted that their own views or activities had been shaped by the pronouncements of celebrities.[9]

Fans use stars' names to identify their preferred styles. Many women have asked their hairdressers for a Princess Di cut, and many men have told corporate fashion consultants that they want to look like Lee Iacocca. Fans have fun speculating on who will be the next Marilyn Monroe. Television personalities, popular musicians, movie stars, fashion models, athletes, and other entertainers have become a commonly shared public experience, especially in the United States.

The obsession with renown extends to the famous themselves. Andy Warhol opined that the best thing about being famous was having the chance to meet other famous people. "Everybody wants to be Cary Grant," said Cary Grant. "Even *I* want to be Cary Grant."[10]

The Intensity of Fame in Modern Society

Some fandoms give individuals space to express silly or trivial feelings, while feeling secure within a group. The seventy-five members of the Princess Kitty Fan Club pay homage to Princess Kitty, "the smartest cat in the world," who can (supposedly) play the piano, slam-dunk a basketball, count, and jump hurdles. The Mr. Ed fan club, named after the talking horse of television fame, has a thousand members and lists "betterment of the world" as its goal.[11]

British football fans use fandom to vent aggression and racism and to exercise a sense of power. Young fans attend away games to get out of town and enjoy a day away from their parents. In many competitions the two groups of fans wear different colors, have different accents, and identify with different local cultures. They scream at each other, exchange racial epithets, and, in some cases, incite fights. Sports teams and leagues cultivate rivalries to help their fans feel different or special, to give their fans something to dislike, or to help fans indulge in vicarious vendettas and power plays.[12]

Fandom often involves collective hostility toward stars, rather than unalloyed worship and approval. The pianist Glenn Gould, who gave up concertizing, described the audience as a hostile force whose "primal instinct was for gladiatorial combat." Presidents, athletes, movie stars, singers, and members of the British royal family are criticized by millions every day. Joey West published the *I Hate Madonna Jokebook*. The *Washington Post* ran a contest that encouraged readers to concoct humorous and elegant put-downs of celebrities. The Internet has led to a proliferation of celebrity "death pools," such as the Ghoul Pool, where people bet which famous individuals will die next. Fred and Judy Vermoral, in their study of fandom, noted: "we were astonished by the degree of hostility and aggression, spoken and unspoken, shown by fans towards stars. Later we realized this was one necessary consequence of such unconsummated, unconsumable passion."[13]

Fans take pleasure in judging presidents, leaders, and famous entertainers by especially harsh and oversimplified standards. In the realm of the stars prejudice is given free reign to rule opinion. Fans can let off critical steam, or express vicarious love, without fear of repercussions, and without having to confront the complexity of the moral issues involved. Jonathan Swift noted that "Censure is the Tax a Man pays to the Publick for being eminent."[14]

Fans use stars to play out their illusions, to distract themselves from daily life, and to express their emotions. The outpouring of sympathy on the death of Princess Diana raises the question of whether and why so many people really cared. To what extent was the outpouring of grief for Diana a cloaked expression of misery in the mourners' own lives or a vicarious release of frustrations? Tinseltown Studios, in Anaheim, California, charges customers $45 for the privilege of being treated as a star; the employees act as cheering crowds and pursuing paparazzi.[15]

A forty-two-year old woman remarked about Barry Manilow: "I suppose it's the same kind of thing people get out of religion. I can't really explain it more than that. But they obviously get something from God to help them through their lives. And Barry is—maybe I shouldn't say it, but it's the way I feel—he's the same sort of thing. He helps me through my life." This same woman claims she thinks of Barry while making love to her husband, only to cry afterward when she realizes that Barry is not there. Another fan refuses to sleep with her husband altogether, ostensibly on the grounds that her husband is not Barry

Manilow. Another fan, named Jane, said, "I think if a nuclear war did happen I'd be thinking: Is Boy George safe?"[16]

In short, ours is a culture steeped in fame. Modern talk show hosts, such as Oprah Winfrey, have daily audiences ranging from 10 to 20 million people. The Barbara Walters interview with Monica Lewinsky was watched by over 70 million Americans, a record for a news program, if it may be called that. Graceland draws more visitors per year—750,000—than does the White House. Boris Yeltsin, when he visited America, asked as he stepped off the plane: "Do you think O. J. did it?" Michael Jordan, the subject of seventy books and one of the most widely recognized figures in the world, is an industry unto himself. In 1998 *Fortune* magazine estimated his career net economic impact at $10 billion.[17]

In the United States there are over 3,000 Halls of Fame. Since the Hall of Fame for Great Americans was initiated in 1901, Halls have been developed for baseball players, rock-and-roll stars, accountants, dog mushers, marbles champions, shuffle board players, pickle-packers, and police officers. Bowlers alone have thirty Halls of Fame for their sport.[18]

Fame has multiplied in virtually all endeavors and has taken on many new forms, of which celebrity is only one manifestation. We have famous musicians, artists, writers, designers, architects, scientists, inventors, charitable benefactors, cooks, critics, fashion models, CEOs, and even economists. Although top scientists cannot compete with Harrison Ford for widespread visibility, they receive recognition from newspapers, scientific journals, peers and colleagues, graduate students, the next generation of scientists, and, occasionally, the general public. "High culture fame" and "low culture fame" have grown together.

Fame-seeking, celebrity, and fandom are deeply rooted psychological phenomena, existing in most societies, but they are amplified and facilitated by commercial market economies and modern technologies. The modern American notions of fame and celebrity date from the 1920s and 1930s, when radio, the recording industry, and motion pictures gave stars an unparalleled ability to reach wide audiences. Today, television, the compact disk, and the Internet give fans further assistance in finding, following, and enjoying their stars from a distance.

Fame has become the ideological and intellectual fabric of modern capitalism. Ours is an economy of fame. Our culture is about the commodification of the individual and the individual image.

FAME VERSUS MERIT

As we will see in later chapters, a market economy separates fame from merit in at least three regards. First, although the fame of some stars is good for society, the fame of others is bad. Fans do not always choose the stars whose fame brings the greatest social benefit.

Second, fans do not always get the stars they want. Fame markets sometimes malfunction, even if we take fan preferences as the standard of merit. The "herd behavior" of crowds may cause stars to rise and fall with excess rapidity. Fans may not be able to coordinate around the stars they truly desire, as I will explain in the next chapter. Or partisans may "overcrowd" fanships, causing less than enough privacy for stars and damaging their creativity.

Third, the famous often fall short of desirable moral and aesthetic standards. Many "heroes" are unadmirable, excessively sensationalistic, or simply boring and untalented. In other cases, the most famous creator in an area may be an admirable and talented producer, but simply not the best of his or her genre. Is the super-famous Andrew Wyeth really better than Jasper Johns or Roy Lichtenstein?

I do not seek to debate who are the best painters, or even whether there is an objective answer to that question. I therefore give two value-free interpretations to this third separation of fame and merit. Under the first interpretation, the distribution of fame will not correspond to *any* prevailing conceptions of aesthetic merit. Partisans of realism and partisans of abstract art will, for instance, both believe that fame and merit are separated. Under the second interpretation, fame will not match the consensus of experts about quality in a given area. If those experts were to try to control the fame-generating process, economic constraints would not allow them to promote reputations in proper proportion to merit.

The separation of fame and merit is a central dilemma for any evaluation of a modern market economy. A system based on voluntary exchange does not reward merit with a concomitant degree of recognition. To assess this reality, I step back and ask some fundamental questions about how fame is produced. Specifically, why are fame and merit so frequently separated? What principles govern who becomes famous and why? Does fame-seeking behavior provide an invisible hand that harmonizes individual and social interests, or do fame markets corrupt social discourse and degrade our culture? Most centrally, what are the implications of modern fame for creativity, privacy, and morality?

PLATO AND THE REPUBLIC OF DECEPTION

The writings of Plato, who virulently opposed the idea of a competitive market in praise, provide the foil for this book. In the dialogues *Protagoras, Crito, Ion, Phaedrus,* and the *Republic,* Socrates attacks individuals who teach and praise for pay—the Sophists—and criticizes praise aimed at entertaining the general public.

Book 11 of Homer's *Odyssey* disturbed Plato. Odysseus meets heroes, such as Achilles, leading a dark and gloomy existence in the underworld, despite their brave and meritorious deeds on earth. Plato's Myth of Er, presented in book 10 of the *Republic,* rewrites this tale with a different ending. When Er travels to the underworld he meets contented heroes and tortured villains. Plato, who used the underworld as a moral parable of punishment and reward, disapproved of how Homer used it to tell a story.

Contrary to Homer, Plato rejected the idea of a competitive praise economy and called for the banishment of the poets, the traditional conduit for Greek praise. Poets praise heroes to entertain their audiences, rather than to offer the appropriate rewards for great deeds. As a result, poets fail to instruct because they must imitate the tastes of their audience to keep their listeners. Philosopher-Kings, Plato's wise and benevolent rulers, will serve as the gatekeepers: "Only so much of poetry as is hymns to gods or celebration of good men should be admitted into a city."[19]

Plato's works are (among other things) an attempt to reform an economy of praise and to restore the link between language and truth. Although most modern commentators reject Plato's belief in comprehensive censorship, the Platonic critique of a free market in praise and fame continues to prove influential, from left-wing thinkers such as Jürgen Habermas to neo-conservatives such as Allan Bloom.

I seek to revise Plato by providing an alternative vision, emphasizing how market-produced praise sparks creativity and achievement. Despite the considerable imperfections of a market in renown, my view of commercialized fame is largely an optimistic one. Markets increase the supply of star performances and the supply of fame with remarkable facility. The offer of praise is a relatively inexpensive means of payment; fame is a "cheap date" for the fans. We use fame to reward and control stars, thus drawing forth a dazzling array of diverse and creative performances. Fame mobilizes the human propensity to talk in support of great achievements.

Ironically, the famous themselves may be the most likely to lose from fame-generating institutions. Socially beneficial fame-seeking often harms the achiever. The famous live under stress and many die young. The quest for approval sometimes becomes a weakness or an addiction, rather than a means of achieving satisfaction. Bernard Mandeville's theme of private vices, public benefits thus can be converted into a tale that Mandeville's opponents would have found morally fitting. The selfish behavior of fame-seekers rebounds to the benefit of society but often gives the fame-seekers little in return. Fame-seekers are often the biggest losers precisely when they appear to reap the largest gains.[20]

A fame-intensive society is a society full of illusions, but deception is an important part of creativity, whether the deceptions be in the mind of the creator or in the mind of the audience. In an earlier book, *In Praise of Commercial Culture*, I portrayed the vitality of the market's influence on contemporary music, art, and literature. I presented the capitalist market economy as a vital framework for supporting a plurality of artistic visions, providing new and satisfying creations, helping consumers and artists refine their tastes, and paying homage to the past by reproduction and dissemination.

At the same time, however, critics support the philosophy of cultural pessimism, which tells us that contemporary culture is failing or in decline. Only the market can support so much successful and diverse carping. Cultural pessimism is itself an illusion that comes from the successful proliferation of creativity. Art cannot be expected to mirror truth, and criticism, as a form of creative art, will not necessarily reflect the truth either. The actions of fans, stars, and critics, taken collectively, create a culture of idol, myth, and make-believe.

This book on fame continues the theme put forth in the commercial culture book that successful societies are full of false beliefs. The widespread production of fame requires that ideas and images are distributed by the market in accord with their private profitability rather than their social use. Plato was correct in believing that the market in ideas would not produce "Truth" with a capital T, but he did not recognize that competing illusions could prove superior to centrally enforced Truth.

Ironically, Plato was himself a primary practitioner of mimesis and illusion, despite his frequent criticisms of those very principles. Plato advances images, narratives, and moral tales to make his own principles more persuasive. The tale of the shadows in the cave in the *Republic* stands as a metaphor for Plato's view of elusive truth. In Plato's parable, man is likened to a cave dweller who spends his time viewing shadows, rather than perceiving the world accurately. Individuals are blinded by the sun, Plato's metaphorical symbol for the truth, when they step outside the cave. The philosopher should strive to make man aware of the sun, so that truth may be served.

Plato was adept at manipulating images to hold our attention and entertain us. He is the lead Sophist of them all and he offers us another set of illusions and metaphors. The tale of the cave is false, but it serves to instruct the Philosopher-Kings. The parable of the cave is a competitively marketed tale, just like the poetry of Homer, which Plato professed to despise. The ultimate metaphor comes when Plato writes in the voice of his teacher Socrates. Plato mimes the voice of another, removes himself from direct responsibility for his doctrines, and creates an additional layer of (delightful) illusion. Just as with contemporary celebrities, the fame of Plato's creations comes not from their merit as absolute truth, but from their ability to instruct and entertain us.[21]

2 | Why Fame Is Separated from Merit

SNOWBALL EFFECTS

The collective aspect of fandom gives rise to snowball effects. Especially in the realm of popular celebrity, each fan looks to what other fans will do. Many fans want to share their stars with other fans, or will accept a variety of stars, provided that others are willing to do the same. Once a performer shows signs of ascent, many fans will jump on the bandwagon and the performer may achieve stardom virtually overnight. Some fans may even support performers they don't really like, to go along with the group and gain approval from their friends, an example of Timur Kuran's "preference falsification." The Spice Girls became famous in a very short time, once they broke into the market.[1]

When snowball effects are present, very small differences in initial success can lead to very large differences in final fame. A star who experiences a favorable snowball effect early in his or her career can become much more renowned than a comparable performer who does not. The small initial burst of support for fame can lead to cumulative and self-reinforcing support over time. The collective nature of fandom, through this mechanism, helps separate fame from actual achievement.

When the Monkees appeared on the musical scene, they traded upon being an American version of the Beatles, albeit of lower quality. Their initial hit singles established their reputation and made their name a household word; once it was expected that the Monkees would succeed, fans and critics scurried to pay attention. The Monkees then got a television show of their own, which further promoted their fame. Even today, most Americans have heard of the Monkees, although in terms of musical merit they were hardly leading lights. Instead, they had some talent and started under favorable conditions, later parleying initial successes into publicity and wider fame.

Fame bubbles can burst as quickly as they formed. Once a performer falls out of favor, and decline is apparent, many fans lose interest and stop purchasing the product. Fans see that the collective fandom benefits are disappearing and they turn to substitutes with comparable or perhaps superior talents. In popular music, performers on the wane rapidly discover they cannot get airtime on the radio or lucrative new recording contracts.

Many fame-producing institutions serve to strengthen reputational snowballs. Fan clubs entice individuals into making fan collectivities larger and stronger, thereby generating cumulative support for their favored performers. To produce the public good of fandom, fan clubs provide activist fans with favorable newsletter publicity, chances to meet the stars, inside gossip, and the power to regulate the access of other, lesser fans. The success of these tactics has no intrinsic link to the merit of the star, even when merit is defined as what the fans desire.

Stars and their distributors try to generate fame snowballs in their favor. Authors and their publishers invest in media blitzes to get onto the bestseller lists, which induce additional purchases of the book. Stars buy advertisements to make themselves the "focal" performer and the center of attention. When fandom begets more fandom, performers will subsidize fans for some initial attention, hoping to create public momentum in their favor.

Many rock groups sell concert tickets at especially low prices, even when that means buyers must wait in long lines. The low prices and queues favor younger buyers, who have less money and who do not mind queuing. Young fans—especially those willing to wait in line—contribute more to rock-and-roll fandom than do older fans. Older fans are less likely to buy the album and they do not usually have a school-based audience of peer-conscious friends.[2]

Snowball effects arise during the course of performances as well. British football teams have set up well-defined ends, or terraces, where hometown fans congregate and cheer, mingle and socialize, plot rowdy activities, indulge in special cultures of dress and song, and feed on each others' enthusiasm. The home crowds treat supporters of the visiting team rudely, or even attack them, to drum up support for the local players. Concert attendees stand, cheer, whistle, clap, and encourage others to do the same. Rock-and-roll fans light matches to call for an encore. Sports fans try to start "human waves" of coordinated standing and arm waving.

WHY MASS CULTURE IS OVERSIMPLIFIED
The mobilizing and coordinating tactics behind collective fandom increase the relative stature of simplistic heroes. The point

is not just that many fans have "low" or degraded tastes. Rather, no matter how good or bad the level of mass taste, a disproportionate number of stars will cluster in the "lower" end of the range.

Large numbers of people can coordinate more easily on relatively obvious and simple matters. Fans, like other large groups, can coordinate their members only to a limited degree. Successful groups make the coordination problem focal, relatively visible, and relatively simple in nature. Thomas Schelling, who originated the idea of focal points, gives the example of two people who agree to meet in New York City but do not specify the place. They are more likely to converge if they head to a well-known and obvious destination, such as the large clock at Grand Central Station, than if they choose a more obscure address or locale. Grand Central Station may not be the most convenient place to meet, but people expect they can coordinate on it.

For similar reasons, fan norms for fame tend to be simple and blunt, rather than detailed and complex. If many fans seek to coordinate around a star performer, the standard for choosing that star must be visible, easy to observe, and easy to evaluate. Mass culture therefore oversimplifies moral and aesthetic issues, even relative to the views of its constituent fans. The mobilization and coordination of large fan groups lowers the level of subtlety and complexity in our culture. Fans do not always prefer the simpler and more obvious stars, but as with Schelling's example of Grand Central Station, that is what they can coordinate around.[3]

Stars try to stand out and mark their "obviousness" for fans, to become focal personalities. Dennis Rodman made himself a widespread topic of conversation. He has led the NBA in rebounding (often by a wide margin), dyed his hair orange and green, and picked fights both on the court and off it. He has drawn attention to himself and become a focal point for fans seeking an anti-authoritarian high achiever as an idol. Basketball players of comparable or superior merits, but whose skills are more evenly distributed (not just confined to rebounding prowess), have a harder time achieving fame, especially if their behavior is less conspicuous. Rodman, although never one of the five best players in the NBA, has been one of the five most famous during his career and a leading recipient of endorsement income.

Music stars use haircuts, styles of dress, and outrageous gimmicks to make themselves focal; Alice Cooper dressed up in drag and Ozzie Osbourne bit off the head of a bat in concert. Jim Morrison, leader of The Doors, once said, "if Spiro Agnew stands for law and order, all right, say I stand for sex. Chaos. Movement without meaning. Cop baiting. Fifty-two week paid vacations with double over-time every year." Stars who reflect or create focal qualities tend to achieve more fame than other performers of comparable or superior talent. When stars first become well known, they are told not to act like their real selves and not to demonstrate too much complexity or real emotion. The star should not step too far outside the persona presented to the public. Staying "in character" is regarded as "safer" and "relatively easy to manage."[4]

Violence is a common and effective focal point. What is more extreme and more visible than killing people with great brutality? It is no wonder that so many movie heroes, such as Arnold Schwarzenegger, dispatch their enemies with so much élan. Some fans feel a visceral attraction to any kind of violence, but the focal qualities of extreme examples of violence—murder

Why Fame Is Separated from Merit

and mayhem—attract even more fan interest. Only excessive violence commands the constant attention of the audience.[5]

The same culture that glorifies violence will use peacefulness as a focal point for many of its heroes. We now take cross-Atlantic aviation for granted, but in the time of Charles Lindbergh it stood for peace and international cooperation. Lindbergh was linked to these goals, and they provided an ideological base for his fame, at least until he accepted a medal from the Nazis in the late 1930s. Although a single culture promotes contrasting ideals—violence and peace—the underlying processes are consistent. Fame-intensive cultures glorify whichever ideals or symbols can be translated into marketable focal points, whether they be positive or negative, traditional or modern. James Joyce has become famous for his obscurity and inaccessibility; *Time* magazine put him on its cover in 1939, precisely for being so difficult to read.[6]

The most famous figures usually represent more than one focal quality at a time—often to different audiences—thus broadening their appeal. Ernest Hemingway was famous as a sportsman, a virile man, an exposer of sham, an arbiter of taste, a world traveler, a bon vivant, an "insider," a stoic and battle-scarred veteran, and a heroic artist. Princess Diana symbolized beauty, domesticity, aristocracy, rags-to-riches, independence, motherhood, and androgyny all at once, to varying groups of followers.[7]

Sometimes a relevant focal quality is accidental or even tragic, as is the case with the scientist Stephen Hawking, who suffers from Lou Gehrig's disease and is confined to a wheelchair. Hawking stands out from the crowd of other physicists, even if his contributions are not the most important. Christopher Reeve, the actor who played Superman, has gained more fame since a horse-riding accident paralyzed him from the neck down. Reeve will remain known for his injury more than for his acting skills, even though he has an accomplished record in the theater. In fact after Reeve's injury he received more acting offers than his flagging career had brought in before.[8]

Premature death, especially under unusual or bizarre circumstances, contributes to the prominence of a star. James Dean, Marilyn Monroe, John F. Kennedy, Buddy Holly, Che Guevara, Selena, Amelia Earhart, River Phoenix, Karen Silkwood, Sharon Tate, Rudolf Valentino, Jim Morrison, Bob Marley, Sid Vicious, Karen Carpenter, Freddie Mercury, Roberto Clemente, Kurt Cobain, Princess Diana, and many others have achieved higher status through their premature or tragic demise. In the late 1970s Elvis's Graceland was a rundown estate near bankruptcy but now it is a leading money-maker and tourist attraction. The sales of rap star Notorious BIG skyrocketed when the artist was murdered in 1997. HIV-positive status made Magic Johnson more famous than he otherwise would have been.

Death often brings stars even more fame. In the process of mourning dead stars, many fans elevate them to a higher symbolic position. The fans imbue the performer with an air of grand tragedy, and consequently the star stands out among his or her contemporaries. Since the star can no longer fail, fans can pour out their emotions without risk of future disappointment. Jimi Hendrix, who himself died young, remarked about stardom, "Once you are dead you are made for life."[9]

Death boosts fame most when the death story matches the image that the star embodied during his or her life. Vincent van Gogh, renowned for his bohemian and anti-establishment lifestyle, became even more famous when he cut off his ear and committed suicide. The fame of Georges Seurat, who died at the age of thirty-one from an aneurysm, did not receive a similar boost. Princess Diana, widely viewed as a victim of media snooping during her life, died in a manner consistent with her public persona and thus attracted an especially high degree of attention.[10]

Some focal qualities are rooted in family identities. The Kennedys, the Fondas, and the Rockefellers all achieve greater fame by being part of well-known clans. In the intellectual sphere, famous families include James and John Stuart Mill, William and Henry James, the Bach family of composers, and the Bernoulli family of mathematicians.

A star's ability to represent a given group, nationality, or constituency further coordinates fandom and increases that star's fame. The tennis star Henri Leconte was a national hero in France even though he would have been just another very good player in the United States. The chess player Murray Chandler is well known among New Zealanders although he does not come close to matching the skills of the world's top competitors. The boxing match between Max Schmeling and Joe Louis was seen as a confrontation between Nazi ideals of Aryanism and African-American ideals of freedom and equality. The world of eighteenth-century French opera pitted the aesthetic styles of Gluck against those of Piccini; in nineteenth-century Germany it was Wagner versus Brahms; and in 1960s England it was the Mods versus the Rockers. Fans of each promoted their preferred aesthetic while seeking to recruit others to the common cause. Publicity skyrocketed in each case.

Gayness, or appeal to gayness, has become a frequent marker of fame in the latter part of this century. Maria Callas projected a sensuous androgyny and cultivated an enthusiastic and influential network of gay male fans. Judy Garland had an image of being misunderstood and maintaining a false exterior. These stars became focal points for homosexual admirers. The Olympic swimmer Greg Louganis boosted his fame when he admitted his homosexuality. *Ellen*, a television show about a lesbian starring a self-professed lesbian, has become one of the best-known programs of the 1990s, even though it was not popular enough to prevent cancellation in 1998.

THE EXCLUSIVITY OF FANDOMS

Successful fan networks produce status for their fans as well as for the star. Exclusivist fans try to project images as non-conformists, hope to validate their self-esteem by being different, or simply wish to avoid the crowds associated with patronizing the truly famous. Fan networks do not usually try to include everybody, but instead exclude some individuals and portray them as outsiders.[11]

Many science fiction fans resent the intrusion of *Star Trek* fans at their conventions; they refer to "the Barbarian Invasion," which supposedly started in the late 1970s. The 1997 Rolling Stones tour attracted mostly older fans, who came to relive memories without feeling the intrusion of the present. One Charles Schwab stockbroker at a show happily noted that his teenage kids were at home "in blessed ignorance. This is *my thing*."[12]

The early Elvis Presley built his reputation upon his unacceptability to the older generation. Young fans who listened to Elvis found themselves chastised or punished. Many parents banned Elvis records outright, although they could not control what came over the radio or what a young fan heard at a friend's house. Had the early Elvis been accepted by parents, some of his younger fans would have rejected him, given that

Elvis fandom was viewed as a sign of youth and rebellion. Elvis fans did not want to share their star with others, especially members of a more conservative older generation.

These exclusionary practices can lower the quality of performances. Elvis, at least early in his career, took deliberate action to keep away "square" fans by engaging in outrageous behavior, at least by the standards of the time.

Fans do not always trust stars to stick to their initial core program and image; this makes fans reluctant to commit their support. Fans fear that their stars eventually will take advantage of their loyalties. Once Elvis sold his product to juveniles and earned large profits, he turned around in the 1960s and courted the establishment. He had nowhere else to go with his anti-establishment approach so he sought out a larger, more mainstream audience. Many of the earlier fans found that their fandom, their records, and their investments in loyalty were devalued by Elvis's overtures to a broader audience. The star will first promise one thing and then do another, as his or her career interests change.[13]

Many stars try to signal to their core fans that they will remain faithful to their initial programs and images. Fringe stars, for instance, seek to precommit to broader social unacceptability, to ensure the loyalty of their anti-establishment and rebellious followers. Basketball player Dennis Rodman has pursued such a strategy by dressing in drag, throwing tantrums, kicking cameramen, and aggressively publicizing his bisexuality. Fans who prize Rodman's anti-authoritarianism do not worry that he will ever be placed on a postage stamp or embraced by conservative Christians.

The requisites needed to commit to an image, or to exclude some fans, often run counter to merit. Some stars end up being excessively crude or outrageous, even relative to what their core supporters would like to see. The core supporters may prefer the crudeness, given the alternative of widespread acceptability (and thus the destruction of the exclusive network), but the supporters nonetheless might find the crudeness excessive relative to their ideal. Similarly, defenders of high-culture exclusivity often take on elitist trappings that are excessive even by the standards of their admirers. The elitism is necessary to maintain exclusion, but devotees may feel pushed into excess.

Some audiences enjoy being ridiculed and disgraced. One 1950s critic wrote of rock and roll: "The more the music was ridiculed . . . the more firmly wielded together the audience became, and the more desperately it attached itself to [the music]." The same holds true today for heavy metal, death metal, and hard rap. Modern culture is full of anti-heroes and nihilist heroes.[14]

Many heroes promote and revel in their (partial) obscurity. Contemporary forms of digitally produced electronic music, such as techno, jungle, and "drum and bass," hide the performer behind a pseudonym (Aphex Twin, Moby, DJ Spooky, Goldie) and a soundboard. It is considered gauche to promote oneself too heavily in this genre. Instead the musician/creator should DJ in the background, adopt a mysterious name, and cut largely instrumental tracks. Few albums in these fields place the artist's picture on the cover.

The 1980s were the age of the super celebrity, such as Madonna, Eddie Murphy, and Arnold Schwarzenegger. The late 1990s show the opposite trend—many fans eschew stars who become too famous. This tendency has been especially pronounced in music, where first albums are becoming rela-

Why Fame Is Separated from Merit

tively more successful than second or subsequent albums. Performers achieve some initial sales and recognition for a hit and then are abandoned by their fans once they become too popular. It remains to be seen whether this trend will persist, but fame has been a self-deflating bubble in some areas.[15]

Some creators try to manufacture images of partial or total unpopularity. Book blurbs sometimes use negative comments instead of positive ones. A negative review can create more enthusiasm, given the partisan nature of opinion and given that praise is frequently insincere in any case. Many readers want to find authors who share their enemies, believing that "the enemy of my enemy is my friend." On a book by Alexander Cockburn, the publisher, Verso, placed a blurb that read: "new standard of gutter journalism." Andy McSmith had a blurb describing him as "biased, ill-informed, malicious and unpleasant." Verso went further with a poster for its author Doug Henwood. The accompanying blurb read: "You're scum. It's tragic you exist." In each case stars used their unpopularity with one group to market their personas to others.[16]

HOW COMMERCIAL PROMOTION INFLUENCES FAME

Fans' demands for stars do not exclusively determine who becomes famous. Some kinds of stars are more profitable to market than others, and achieve a special renown, disproportionate to underlying fan interest. It is easier for suppliers to make money by promoting Madonna—who produces salable, reproducible outputs like CDs—than to make money by promoting Mother Teresa, who labored with the poor and did not try to sell products to mass audiences. Suppliers, advertisers, distributors, and other intermediaries invest more resources in marketing stars who yield profit.

Stars who are advertised have a much easier time becoming famous than stars who are not. Nine tenths of the time Americans spend with the media is devoted to advertising-supported media, most notably television and radio. Approximately a quarter of television time and a fifth of radio time is taken up by the advertisements themselves. Advertisements fill three fifths of newspaper space and over half of the pages in magazines. I refer to advertising in its many forms—the purchase of praise and favorable publicity—as *praise for sale*.[17]

Payola occurs in many forms, as when record companies pay radio station disc jockeys to promote performers and play their songs on the air. Although payola was outlawed in 1959, payments to station program directors, or exchanges of favors, remain common. In addition, some record companies now (legally) pay radio stations to play their songs, with the announcement that the playing is a paid advertisement.[18]

When the time approaches for the Golden Globe awards, Hollywood studios shower critics with gifts, parties, and out-of-town junkets. Theater, ballet, and musical companies pay critics to write their program notes, hoping to purchase "good will" in return. Record companies pay to have their CDs placed on listening stations in CD stores. Publishers buy larger spreads and favorable publicity from Amazon.com. Newspapers put pressure on their movie critics to write favorable reviews because movie advertisements are a significant source of revenue for the papers. Television advertisers put pressure on networks to shy away from adverse publicity for their products or for their chief executives. Stars reward enthusiastic critics by granting them exclusive interviews or by giving them the chance to write the authorized biography.[19]

Funders sometimes buy the critic outright and vertically integrate. Book clubs, rather than paying outside critics to slant their reviews, hire their own advisory board to select and recommend books to their readers, and then publicize these recommendations in the form of monthly book club selections. The selection may be accompanied by an explanatory newsletter or descriptive blurb, providing favorable publicity. The advisory board members, employed by the book club, have the same incentives as critics "on the take"—they endorse works to boost the profits of the parent company.[20]

Equity Payola

Some performers pay for praise by giving critics a financial stake in their reputations. The songwriting credits to Chuck Berry's "Maybellene" were given in part to the well-known disc jockey Alan Freed. Leonard Chess of Chess Records (Berry's record company) went to Freed with a large selection of material. Chess offered Freed partial songwriting credits on the song of his choice, provided that he would play and promote it. Freed thus had a strong incentive to find, pick, and promote the song with the greatest potential popularity. After listening to hundreds of recordings, Freed picked "Maybellene." Berry became a star, and Freed received royalties. I speak of equity payola when the critic has an ongoing stake in the success of the product, rather than just receiving a one-time cash payment.[21]

Painters give away works to well-placed critics and buyers. Clement Greenberg, the renowned art critic, was accused of accepting free paintings from artists in return for promoting their reputations. Initially, the critic has one reason to praise the artist, to receive an artwork in return. Later, the critic has cause to continue praising the artist, to see the artist's reputation and prices rise as high as possible.[22]

Paintings, especially those by young up-and-coming artists, usually are not sold at the price that would equate market demand to market supply. Gallery owners, often with exclusive dealing rights, create excess demand through low prices and then ration paintings to buyers who will promote the long-run reputation of the artist. The buyer, who now owns an expensive painting, has a direct financial and reputational stake in promoting the artist. The artist and gallery promote their long-term interests by creating and subsidizing highly influential fans. Art insiders have the easiest time buying high-quality works, and the best works usually are sold before a gallery exhibit opens; these practices produce fame for rising artists. The best galleries exhibit paintings not to sell them (typically the buyers are recruited in advance), but rather to publicize the artist, thereby increasing the value of the dealer's unsold stock and publicizing the dealer and the artist. One study of etchers showed that the artists who were skillful at targeted donations and sales attained greater long-run fame than did etchers with less marketing proficiency.[23]

Whose Fame Does Praise for Sale Promote?

Praise for sale favors the fame of stars who profit greatly from an increase in the size of their market. In economic language, it favors the fame of stars whose profits are highly elastic with respect to market demand.

All other things being equal, a larger market makes publicity more profitable, and in that sense praise for sale responds to fan demands. Stars and their promoters try to avoid investing

Why Fame Is Separated from Merit

in futile endeavors or promoting losers, to preserve their profits and their reputations. Nonetheless, praise for sale gives undue weight to the fame of performers with new products, unique products, reproducible products, and products that are easily "equitized," as we will see below. Stars and their intermediaries bid for fame, and the success of these bids depends, in part, on factors incidental to fan assessments of star quality. The scale of commercial promotion for a given star depends on the ability of stars to capture profits through their promotions, not just on fan interest. Fans accept an active but unruly set of commercial servants when they patronize praise for sale.[24]

Praise for sale favors the fame of new musical stars over that of older musical stars. If an advertiser promotes one particular recording of Tchaikovsky's *Pathetique* Symphony, consumers may buy a different recording of the same symphony, given the relatively small differences between performances. If an advertiser promotes Tori Amos, a responsive fan will be more likely to buy a CD by her than one by Michael Jackson. The personality-specific popular music world produces more sharply differentiated products than does the realm of classical music, where skilled orchestras are near-perfect substitutes for each other. For similar reasons, commercial promotion favors the fame of stars with copyright protection or unique personalities. The performer who competes with many close substitutes has less reason to stimulate fan interest, given that fan expenditures might spill over onto the substitutes instead.[25]

Most promotions are aimed at generating new hits, a practice that also augments favors the fame of up-and-coming stars relative to that of older achievers. In many markets, such as books and music, most products flop or barely break even. Producers are trying to find and promote the relatively small number of new products that will "take off" and bring in high profits. Older products already have been classified as successes or failures and do not receive the same promotional effort. The new product has a better chance of becoming the next craze and therefore receives greater promotion. Once a work falls out of favor, or once its copyright has expired, intermediaries lose interest in enhancing the fame of the creator, if they have not done so long before.

Praise for sale favors products and performances that can be reproduced easily. The mass production of Eddie Murphy videos expands his audience without his having to repeat the performance. More copies can be sold without a great increase in cost, since the physical production of the video is not very expensive. Stimulating demand therefore increases Eddie Murphy's profits and praise for sale spreads his fame. Similarly, recorded music and published writing can be reproduced at very low cost, provided that customers for the output can be found. Creators of these products use praise for sale to expand the size of their market and capture more profit.

Artistic reproductions are worth much less than original paintings, which are unique. Reproducibility brings a significant decline in value. Recruiting more buyers among the masses therefore has a weaker effect on profits. Most painters create a relatively small number of works in their lifetimes. Although they draw on previous themes and ideas, they do not enjoy the effortless and exact electronic reproduction that we find in music, movies, or publishing. Most painters court a small network of wealthy buyers instead of aiming at the masses. For this reason, in a commercialized society the fame of recorded musicians, writers, and movie actors and actresses will grow relative to the fame of painters and sculptors. Michelangelo was the most famous Florentine creator in his day, but today Jasper Johns is not as well known as a rock singer of middling success, much less David Bowie or Mick Jagger.[26]

Commercial promotions do not give greatest prominence to the best and most discerning critics. Indeed, many who dispense criticism are not primarily critics, but are famous for other reasons. Howard Stern gives his opinions about movies and music while providing comic dialogue for his listeners and being a star in his own right. Although this combination of functions produces especially potent influence, criticism ends up in the hands of entertainers, rather than in the hands of individuals who know most about the products. The tactics that mobilize critical influence do not necessarily improve the quality of the resulting criticism. Oprah Winfrey typically recommends high-quality novels to her audience, but not all stars have such good critical taste.

Finally, praise for sale favors seekers of praise rather than seekers of praiseworthiness. Performers who love recognition even when they do not deserve it will not hesitate to buy publicity and engage in aggressive self-promotion. Many of these stars, who use fame as a stepping stone to money and sex, embrace payola wholeheartedly. Other performers want to earn respect for their achievements the hard way. They attach little value to fame that is bought, believing instead that fame should be earned through merit and through the sincere admiration of critics and audiences. These performers are less keen to spend money to promote themselves and less eager to seek fame in a commercial market economy.

What Styles Does Praise for Sale Favor?

Praise for sale influences styles of art and performance. More specifically, it has two opposing affects on aesthetic values. First, praise for sale encourages churning: reproduction of the same product and repetition of the same characteristics in different products. Not only does Barbara Cartland have an arrangement with her publisher to print, distribute, and promote many copies of a single book, but she also repeats her basic formulas and ideas in many different books. Composers of country and western songs often perfect a set of chord changes and themes and then produce variants of the basic product at low additional cost. Canaletto painted pictures of Venice for his English clients in great numbers, one after the other, once he had the style mastered. Creators of this kind use promotion to increase the demand for their products and they can meet the surge in demand at relatively low cost. This mechanism favors styles based on mass production, or churning, which tend to be lowbrow in nature.

A second and competing mechanism favors highbrow styles, as defined by the complexity of the aesthetic. Creators who learn more as they produce reap relatively high benefits from promotion. Composers or authors may build up to a great work with a series of intermediate works of lesser greatness, as did Beethoven and Mozart. Artistic achievements in these fields are to some extent cumulative and based on ongoing experience with creation. The steady producer who learns from successive works, and builds these insights into subsequent creations finds praise for sale of relatively high value.

Punk musicians, who are rarely steady producers, do not benefit much from praise for sale. Punk music typically is produced by very young performers who burn out rapidly and cannot produce additional high-quality products for any length of time. Either the creators self-destruct with drugs, as did the Sex Pistols, or their earned wealth assuages their anger and removes their musical rebelliousness, as happened with The Clash. Punk musicians may use payola to achieve initial market access, but they face diminishing returns from outlays intended to stimulate demands for their future products. Given the market conditions they face, it is no surprise that early punk musicians eschewed and mocked commercial advertising.

Equity payola does not produce fame equally for all aspirants. Performers who can easily give critics a stake in their reputations gain in fame, relative to performers who cannot. In particular, equitization favors stars with resalable material products. Many kinds of artists, such as stage actors, do not produce resalable outputs. A critic can hear and observe a soliloquy, or watch a mime, but a critic cannot easily own shares in the product itself. In this regard reputational equity for the live performer differs from that for the painter. The live stage performer cannot easily give critics a financial stake in his or her success and therefore will have a harder time becoming famous than the painter, all other things being equal.

Equity payola favors the fame of performers who can identify and subsidize their most influential promoters. Painters who can identify the relevant opinion-makers can promote their fame (and long-run income) by selling their works to elites. But painters who sell outside of established art centers have a harder time targeting and identifying influential groups because of their distance from the core of opinion. That is why galleries act as intermediaries for painters and why those galleries tend to be geographically clustered.

Equitization, by linking the critic's income to the performer's income, induces many critics to promote mass market strategies for the performer. Leading critics for alternative or indie rock bands often want their favored bands to go commercial and "sell out." David Marsh was a *Rolling Stone* writer who was linked to Bruce Springsteen before Springsteen became extremely famous. Subsequently, Marsh's star rose with Springsteen's, but Springsteen had to make his music more commercial to reap large financial rewards. Rather than objecting to this trend (as did many hard-core fans), Marsh promoted it, knowing it would increase his own fame and income as well. Marsh sought to convince the world that the new, more popular persona did not clash with Springsteen's previous ideals. Marsh had strong reason to do Springsteen's bidding, since he relied on access to Springsteen for his articles and for his status as Springsteen's authorized biographer. Critics are more likely to act in this fashion when they are attached to stars than when they must make their own way without a star's help. Audiences therefore should be suspicious of "insider" critics with close links to stars and should pay special heed to the critical writings of outsiders.

Like performers, critics try to give others a reason to promote their fame. A critic who pans all artists will find that no artist will promote his or her reputation as a critic. Film critics who rave about movies see their names reproduced in advertising blurbs more frequently than critics who are more reserved. In fact, some critics produce a steady stream of praise for nearly all movies, good or bad, in part to have their names appear in movie ads.[27]

Some performers manipulate the style of their product to shift the incentives of critics to pay attention. Richard Posner cites Shakespeare, Nietzsche, Wittgenstein, and Kafka as figures who owe part of their reputation to the enigmatic and perhaps even contradictory nature of their writings. Unclear authors, at least if they have substance and depth, receive more attention from critics and require more textual exegesis. Individual critics can establish their own reputations by studying such a writer and by promoting one interpretation of that writer's work over another. These same critics will support the inclusion of the writer in the canon, to promote the importance of their own criticism. In effect, deep and ambiguous writers are offering critics implicit invitations to serve as co-authors of a broader piece of work. Critics respond by scrutinizing these works more closely and spreading their fame more widely.[28]

In the economics literature, enormous attention is devoted to the vagaries of John Maynard Keynes's *General Theory*. The monetary writings of Milton Friedman or Irving Fisher, far clearer and not inferior as practical guides to monetary policy, do not receive equal attention from historians of thought. It is more difficult to establish a reputation as an interpreter of Friedman than of Keynes.

The ambiguous political message of George Orwell's *Nineteen Eighty-Four* has helped cement his fame. Critics on the left have argued that Orwell's dystopia represents the fascist capitalist state, and have pointed to Orwell's socialism in support of this interpretation. Critics on the right have claimed Orwell as an insightful critic of communism and left-wing totalitarianism. The plasticity of Orwell's writings allows them to be used on both sides of the political spectrum. Had Orwell specified the political message of his works more clearly, he might today be less famous, and *Nineteen Eighty-Four* would have become a purely partisan touchstone in a political debate rather than a source of interpretative discussion. Similarly, as the historian François Furet argued, the French Revolution achieved such great fame because it allows for multiple political interpretations. Both conservatives and revolutionaries can cite the revolution to make their points.[29]

IS THE SEPARATION OF FAME AND MERIT UNDESIRABLE?

The separation of fame and merit is not necessarily a negative development. Fans *choose* the separation of fame from merit, in large part, because they benefit from it. As the above examples suggest, the same processes that separate fame and merit allow more fame to be produced. Fans, and stars, accept a weaker link between fame and merit in return for a greater quantity and diversity of fame.

The promotion of commercially successful stars, however unappealing to some outside observers, represents a relatively cheap way of interesting corporations in fame production. The production of large-scale renown requires the cooperation of outside parties, such as advertisers and promoters. So many people cooperate in the production of fame only because a lot of money can be made through the process, and that fact in turn increases attention to what is profitable. The oversimplifications of modern fame are part of the price we voluntarily pay for the mobilization of large audiences at low cost. Commercial promotions do not give fans the stars they want most in absolute terms, but they do give fans the stars they are willing to pay for.

Fans can limit the biases of praise for sale when they so wish. Rather than following the advice of mainstream radio stations and advertisements when choosing the music they buy, fans can generate their own information. They can borrow

Why Fame Is Separated from Merit

recordings from friends, check recordings out from the library, consult academic critics, or demand that music shops allow listeners to hear compact disks before purchasing them, as do many European shops and the Blockbuster chain in the United States. In essence, fans can limit the impact of payola by informing themselves.

In some cases fans do not know that the critics are being paid to offer their praise, and praise for sale represents a kind of fraud. But in most cases praise for sale succeeds for other reasons. Even when fans know that publicity is "bought," they may value the information received and respond by buying the product. I am more likely to buy the compact disks played on the Tower Records listening stations, even though I know that the time has been been bought by record and CD promoters. I have a chance to hear the music and if I like it I will buy it. Few critics of commercial culture hesitate to check out the "New Books" table at Borders or Barnes & Noble, even though publishers pay to have their books put on it.

Promotional campaigns signal the belief of distributors or critics that a product will prove popular. I assume that an advertised CD is "hot," and therefore of potential interest. Furthermore, both distributors and critics wish to protect and extend the value of their reputations. They may be willing to accept payola, but they would rather accept payola for popular products than for unpopular products. A critic who continually praises inferior products will lose reputation and audience attention. Suppliers therefore find it cheaper to purchase praise for potential hits than for obvious duds; it is easier to buy a critic when the product is a plausible one. When fans see payola, they respond favorably by expecting a successful and popular product.[30]

Even though payola does not match fan preferences exactly, it may be the best source of information that fans have, relative to the cost of its acquisition. Praise for sale brings numerous and enthusiastic promotions to fans, often for free. Sometimes fans are paid to see, listen to, or read messages of praise. Fans have entire industries at their doorstep, trying to figure out which promotions will best create profitable new stars. These commercial forces often promote new products with greater skill and interest than would "objective" critics with no financial interest at stake.

In many cases stars purchase publicity to make themselves the "focal" performer and center of attention. Fans do not care if the critic praises for pay, they simply want to follow the star with the greatest amount of publicity of a certain kind. Commercial praise can create or cement a star's fame by placing that star in the public eye. Praise for sale is then especially likely. When the time comes to single out the next star, fans are happy to receive an outside recommendation for free, rather than paying to control the choice directly.

We often observe fans choosing praise for sale, even when more informed sources are available for free. The Tower Records chain gives away a free periodical of music reviews entitled *Pulse*. The magazine is highly literate, hires excellent critics, and eschews mainstream products. *Pulse* maintains standards of quality and integrity to keep its audience, and offers wiser musical judgments than do Tower window displays. The window advertisements are prominent at Tower store entrances, and target a less discriminating class of customer. Fans choose either the window displays or *Pulse* for guidance, depending on their purposes and musical seriousness. By distributing *Pulse* for free, Tower Records encourages fans to choose the level of commercial influence which suits them best.

If fans find that the biases of commercial promoters loom too large, they can hire promoters through *subscription* to serve fan ends. When fans pay the entire bill, they exercise a dominant influence over their sources of information and evaluation. In almost Marxian fashion, subscription finance allows fans to construct their culture as a conscious project, employing critics to assist them in this endeavor. Critics try to satisfy fans—their funders—rather than serving outside commercial interests such as distributors, advertisers, and promoters.

Fans choose to pay higher ticket prices to watch a movie in a theater that does not interrupt their viewing pleasure with advertisements. Internet users pay subscription fees to avoid the promotions that many Web services flash on the screen.

The buyer of this book—which is not funded by advertisements—is willing to pay its price for knowledge about the economics of fame. *People* magazine, funded largely by advertisements, also has much to say about fame, and sells for a lower price, but its mode of analysis would not suit many of my readers. When it comes to the economics of fame, not all readers want to suffer the compromises and simplifications that the need for advertising revenue imposes on the content of *People* magazine.

The medium of telephone conversations illustrates similar tradeoffs between expense and control over content. Most telephone speakers do not want advertising to intrude on their phone calls and they would rather pay a fee for their phone services. In principle, telephone conversations could be funded by advertising. And in fact some European telephone companies have begun experiments along these lines (U.S. companies are developing similar ideas). In one part of Sweden the speaker has the option of calling for free, but must hear an advertisement while waiting to be connected, and the speakers must pause for an advertisement after every three minutes of talk. Whether or not this idea catches on is beside the point. Fans will choose the mix of control, convenience, and price that best serves their interests.[31]

Since fans can reject and control advertising at will, subscription finance serves as a benchmark for understanding the role of advertising and commercial promotion in mass culture. Subscription finance has many desirable properties, but it is too expensive to take over the entire market for criticism and star-making. Through the use of subscription finance, fans can repel promotions that they would find especially harmful, but continue to have access to those advertisements that they find tolerable or beneficial.

Marshall McLuhan pointed out that a medium shapes its messages, but he neglected to emphasize the role of fans and customers in choosing the medium and the kind of shaping that will occur. Competition does not eliminate the biases of fame-producing media, but it does allow fans to select which biases they will encounter and therefore to minimize the costs of those biases. McLuhan took communications media to be autonomous structural forces, with a life of their own. In reality, media must compete with each other and mold their messages to either meet consumer demands or shape consumer demands in the most profitable way possible. Consumers and fans choose the medium, and how it is funded, depending on what kind of messages they want to hear.

CELEBRITY ENDORSEMENTS

At first glance, celebrity endorsements seem to reflect the ultimate corruption of public discourse. The star is simply *paid* to supply the endorsement; he or she is usually not an expert on the product. In Canada Wayne Gretzky has endorsed hockey sticks, but he also has endorsed insurance, toys, and a breakfast cereal. A development company in Georgia sells condominiums as "Jack Nicklaus homes." The estate of Salvador Dali collects royalties from the scent that bears his name. Dan Marino, the Miami Dolphins quarterback, has been paid in part with an equity share in LaRussa Italian foods, whose products he promotes. The architect Michael Graves licenses his name to Bloomingdales for use in selling kettles and carrier bags. Dick Clark sells his voice to telemarketing services. Michael Jackson received millions of dollars for endorsing Pepsi-Cola, even though he does not drink it. Michael Jordan has endorsed dozens of products, from aprons to pencil sharpeners. It is estimated that 20 percent of all American television commercials include a famous person. These individuals become more famous through their endorsement activities, without any apparent link to their merit.[32]

I view celebrity endorsements more favorably. Most endorsements support the production and distribution of fame, to the benefit of stars, companies, and fans. Celebrity endorsements help coordinate fans, and help fans spend their money more effectively.

When the endorsed product is not very well known, the endorsing star certifies its quality. The star links his or her reputation to that of the product, thereby indicating to consumers that the product is OK to buy, rather than faulty or noxious. In effect, the star (and his or her agent) serves as a delegated monitor for the vast national market of consumers. Who better to act as a guide than a face and image that everyone knows? In other words, the fame market, and the existence of the famous, allow other markets to work more smoothly.

Stars may not be experts on the products they endorse, but the agents of stars are experts in making money for stars. Stars post their fame as a guarantee or bond to ensure their reliability as endorsers; a star who consistently endorsed poor products would become less popular with fans. The star's agent therefore steers stars away from the "wrong products" or products that convey "the wrong image." If a fan knows something about the star, the fan can infer what kind of products that star will endorse. The fan is then more likely to buy those products, making the fan happier, the company more profitable, and the star more famous.

Other endorsements—especially those for well-known products—serve a function like that of collectible trading cards. Fans seek to consume images of their favorite stars. The marketing of these images through material goods and services—Michael Jordan on posters or on the Wheaties box—supports the coordination of fandom and the dissemination of the star's fame.

General Mills puts Michael Jordan on its Wheaties boxes because it perceives an opportunity to bring Jordan and his fans together; the company sees untapped gains from trade, so to speak. The fans want to offer Jordan more homage and he wants more renown. Putting Jordan's image on the cereal box packages and sells fandom, and fans "buy" the homage at a positive price by switching from other cereals to Wheaties. Wheaties sells Jordan's fame to his fans, just as, when Jordan was still playing professional basketball, the owners of the Chicago Bulls promoted him by selling tickets. The Wheaties box spread the Jordan image to fans who have never seen him play in person or simply wish to offer additional homage to Jordan.

Because of the collective nature of fandom and fame, many fans prefer to buy Jordan images with a Wheaties box than in separate, individualized markets. By paying homage to an athlete through a Wheaties purchase, a fan receives reasonable assurance that other fans are doing the same. Wheaties is a nationally established brand found in most American supermarkets. Especially when the star is not fully established, as Jordan was not in his earlier years, prospective fans want to see that their enthusiasm feeds into a larger collective effort. Purchase of an individualized memento does not bring assurances of an accompanying collective fervor. Since no single memento supplier has the market presence of Wheaties, the memento purchaser receives no assurance that other fans are participating in similar kinds of homage.

When fame is sold to many customers in reproducible form, such as a poster or a compact disk, widespread purchase of the item helps fans coordinate their praise. When Michael Jordan was still playing, if a poster portrayed him slam-dunking, fans cheered more every time he slam-dunked. Jordan responded by slam-dunking more and by developing better slam-dunk moves. The poster company tried to package Jordan fandom in attractive forms, by creating posters with highly motivational images or by portraying great basketball rivalries. Fans responded to the posters that did the best job of spurring Jordan on to the feats they wanted to see, such as ever more spectacular slam-dunks.

Star endorsements serve as a modified form of the wax museum. Rather than setting up wax dummies, as does Madame Tussaud's, Wheaties reproduces Jordan's image on cardboard, and in lieu of charging direct admission, Wheaties asks Jordan fans to switch cereal brands and pay a product premium for consuming his image.

The use of endorsements to coordinate fandom suggests that stars should endorse those products that the star's fans buy, rather than products that the star knows something about. The Jordan image will be marketed by companies—such as Wheaties—that are relatively effective coordinators of Jordan's fans. Similarly, golf stars and tennis stars advertise those commodities that golf and tennis fans tend to buy. That Jim Courier endorses tennis equipment and Rolex watches reflects the wealthy and elite composition of tennis fandom.

In these cases, a company is most willing to pay stars for endorsements when it is competing against roughly similar products. Michael Jordan, in effect, asks fans to give up Corn Flakes to partake in his fan network by purchasing Wheaties. To the extent that fans can switch cereals without sacrificing much in terms of taste, this appeal has a chance of succeeding. If the differences between breakfast cereals were large, we would not expect to see Jordan's image on a cereal box. The cereals would compete in terms of flavor and quality, rather than through star-packaging. But since breakfast cereals are much alike and most people can switch cereals at relatively low cost, putting celebrities on the boxes is a worthwhile endeavor for the cereal companies.

Most economic theories of endorsements, in contrast, predict that we will see star endorsements for products that are unique and sold by powerful monopolists. The theory of "signaling," for instance, predicts that endorsements will be associated most frequently with unique, high-quality products. That theory maintains that companies invest in costly endorsements to prove ("signal") that they have a special product or a significant cost advantage. Similarly, "taste shift" theories of advertising, associated with Thorstein Veblen and John Kenneth

Galbraith, imply a monopolist who earns high profits and can gain by increasing product demand. Although these theories possess merit in many cases, they fail to consider how the market for fame shapes modern advertising and thus they do not offer a complete account of celebrity endorsements.[33]

3 | The New Heroes and Role Models

Critics charge that the commercial generation of fame leads to a society weak in virtue. Daniel Boorstin thinks the concept of transient celebrity is replacing the concept of the true hero, who serves as a role model and exhibits moral leadership. Winston Churchill asked, "Can modern communities do without great men? Can they dispense with hero-worship? Can they provide a larger wisdom, a nobler sentiment, a more vigorous action, by collective processes, than were ever got from Titans? Can nations remain healthy, can all nations draw together, in a world whose brightest stars are film stars?"[1]

To the extent that these worries are valid, the separation of fame and merit is more dangerous than I suggested in the previous chapter. We run the danger that commercially successful heroes induce dangerous forms of mimesis and fail to help citizens coordinate around noble ideals.

In *Parallel Lives,* Plutarch wrote of great men as a kind of looking glass, in which we see how to "adjust and adorn" our own lives. In an essay satirically titled "Live Unknown," he argued that both moral virtue and moral disease should be flaunted to publicize the nature of a good life. Plutarch's polemic, aimed at the Stoics, emphasized the instructional benefits of observing prominent individuals. Fame-seekers demonstrate virtue and set examples for others to follow. In the Stoic account individual introspection suffices to produce knowledge of the good life; for Plutarch, knowledge of the good life requires a public and competitive process of discovery. The contemporary question is whether today's heroes provide a foundation for moral discourse of a desirable kind.[2]

THE CHANGING NATURE OF FAME

Over time, entertainers and sports figures have displaced politicians, military leaders, and moral preachers as the most famous individuals in society, and in some cases, as the most admired. The funeral of Princess Diana attracted far more attention than the funeral of Mother Teresa, held the same week.

An 1898 survey of 1,440 twelve- through fourteen-year-olds asked them the following question: "What person of whom you have ever heard or read would you most like to resemble?" Forty percent chose either George Washington or Abraham Lincoln. Clara Barton, Annie Sullivan (Helen Keller's teacher), Julius Caesar, and Christopher Columbus also received prominent mention. One bicycle racer and one boxer were mentioned, but otherwise sports figures accounted for few of the answers. Seventy-eight percent of the selections came from history, both contemporaneous and past, including politicians, moral leaders, and generals. No entertainers were picked but 12 percent were characters from literature.

Another poll was conducted in 1948 with a comparable number of schoolchildren of similar age. The question read:

"Which one of all these persons that you know or have read about do you want most to be like 10 years from now?" In this survey only a third of the respondents chose historical figures; Franklin Delano Roosevelt topped the list for boys and Clara Barton topped the list for girls. Sports figures accounted for 23 percent, with baseball players Ted Williams and Babe Ruth heading that category. Entertainers accounted for 14 percent, with boys picking radio heroes like Gene Autry and girls preferring movie figures such as Betty Grable. Characters from literature were completely absent. Religious figures fell from 5 percent in 1898 to less than 1 percent in 1948. Figures from comic strips, such as Joe Palooka, were selected much more often than Jesus Christ.[3]

In 1986 *The World Almanac* listed the ten figures most admired by American teenagers in that year, all of whom except Ronald Reagan (himself a former actor) were entertainers:

1. Bill Cosby
2. Sylvester Stallone
3. Eddie Murphy
4. Ronald Reagan
5. Molly Ringwald
6. Chuck Norris
7. Clint Eastwood
8. Rob Lowe
9. Arnold Schwarzenegger
10. Don Johnson

The images on recent U.S. postage stamps—Buddy Holly and Elvis Presley, for instance—further reflect commercializing forces. Postage stamps from the nineteenth century portray and commemorate political and military leaders almost exclusively.

Most early stamps are of George Washington (a few others are of Lincoln), and Washington is portrayed in the pose captured by the painter Gilbert Stuart and immortalized on the dollar bill. The public now clamors for new and different images. After Elvis Presley's death, his fans lobbied to have him put on a stamp. Fans bickered over whether a young, handsome Elvis or an older, fatter Elvis should be used. The subsequent public vote attracted so much attention that the networks televised the press conference for the announcement of the winning stamp.[4]

The proportion of stamps with politicians has fallen over the years and in recent times entertainers have become prominent. Until the late 1960s only two entertainers had made it onto U.S. postage stamps. The 1970s and 1980s combined brought a total of nine entertainers on stamps. The first half of the 1990s has brought thirty-two entertainers on stamps.[5]

At the beginning of this century, political biographies accounted for 46 percent of the sampled magazine biographies published in the United States. By 1940 the figure had fallen to 25 percent. The market share of entertainment biographies picked up most of the slack, moving from 26 percent of the market in 1900 to 55 percent of the market in 1940. In the 1901–1914 period, 77 percent of all entertainment biographies covered "serious" high art. The figure had fallen to 38 percent by the 1920s, and by the time period 1940–41, only 9 percent of the entertainment biographies counted as serious.[6]

Do We Look Up to the Famous?

Modern fame removes the luster from societal role models. Today almost all individuals appear less meritorious, given the commercial incentives for intense media scrutiny. The more we see of our leaders and the more we know about them, the less exalted they appear, even if they are no worse than heroes from times past.

Earlier leaders stood at a greater distance from the citizenry. When Abraham Lincoln was assassinated, people in some parts of the country did not know of his death for up to a month afterward. When Grover Cleveland and Woodrow Wilson underwent serious health crises, the public was kept in the dark. Before the 1920s, most people had never heard the voice of the President, and before the 1950s most people had never seen the President live on television. In the 1930s many Americans did not know that Franklin Roosevelt used a wheelchair. As recently as the 1950s, when Eisenhower was in the White House, journalists did not feel that they should quote the President without his permission. The sexual affairs of John F. Kennedy were not reported, even though many journalists knew about them.[7]

Today, virtually every known fact about Bill Clinton has been reported. We hear about his taste for Elvis Presley, his golf score, and his affair with Monica Lewinsky—in exquisite detail. The ability of Presidents to orchestrate their own images has decreased as information sources have become more competitive and technologies of reproduction have become more acute.

The press, following the wishes of its viewers and readers, devotes special attention to embarrassing moments and gaffes. The modern image of a leader is not Theodore Roosevelt charging up a hill, but rather Jimmy Carter fighting off a rabbit with a canoe paddle, Gerald Ford stumbling and bumping his head, or George Bush vomiting in the lap of the Japanese prime minister. Bill Clinton will be defined forever by his handling of the Monica Lewinsky affair. These images demystify power and produce a culture of disillusionment with politics and moral leadership.[8]

It is no accident that the United States, the country most obsessed with fame and celebrity, gives politicians the least privacy and strips them most of their dignity. Since today's leading politicians are first and foremost celebrities, they can no longer control public access to the details of their lives. From the point of view of the public, celebrities are for primarily for *knowing about* and *talking about.*

Successful politicians must use television and compete with popular culture for audience attention. Leaders therefore court voters by entertaining them and making them feel good. This strategy may increase popularity and win votes, but it diminishes the stock of moral authority a leader can wield. Bill Clinton appealed to the younger generation when he played the saxophone on Arsenio Hall's show, but he also lowered the stature and moral authority of the Presidency.

The increasing weight of short-run political opinion makes the President a moral follower rather than a leader. Political audiences are much larger today than in earlier times, and the scrutiny of those audiences is more intense. Modern polling techniques keep politicians on a relatively short leash. The media, in turn, seek profits; they promote political images that will attract viewers, rather than images that support the dignity of the office.

Contemporary Presidents are deluged with attention, but they find it hard to earn respect, increase their stature, and stake out their place in history. It is hard to imagine any current President reaping the prestige of George Washington. Washington was the target of much criticism during his terms of office, but he later achieved near deification as a statesman and leader.

Between 1800 and 1860, more than four hundred books and articles about his life were published. Writers sometimes referred to Washington as "Him," noted that his mother's name was Mary, and compared him to Jesus Christ. Many Americans had a likeness of Washington's image—a picture, a statuette, a sampler—in their homes. Washington's portrait adorns the dollar bill, and his name has been given to 1 state, 8 streams, 9 colleges and universities, 10 lakes, 7 mountains, 33 counties, and 121 cities and towns. There is a holiday in his honor and many shrines have been erected in his likeness, including the famous Washington Monument in the heart of the nation's capital.[9]

Like the Presidency, most monarchies have fallen in prestige. Commercial fame and celebrity altered the British monarchy in the middle of the nineteenth century, largely because of the invention of photography. Bertie, Prince of Wales and the son of Victoria and Albert, created a worldwide sensation when he visited North America in 1860. People knew what Bertie looked like, how he had grown up, and how he dressed, all because of the camera. In America Bertie was followed around by mobs and eventually had to confine himself to carriages, for fear of danger. Three hundred thousand people turned out to accompany him in Manhattan. The monarchy became better known, but also more familiar and less prestigious.

New technologies for travel and broadcast continued to increase the reach of the monarchy and diminish its stature. In 1903 King Edward VII traveled 8,000 miles to five countries. In 1924 King George V addressed England on the radio. By 1936 the royal family was worrying whether the death of the king would be reported in the morning or afternoon editions of the newspaper. In 1953 the coronation of Queen Elizabeth was televised and watched by 20 million Britons. In 1981, when 750 million people watched the marriage of Charles and Diana, the English monarchy was almost exclusively a public showpiece.[10]

Who Becomes a Leader?

The commercialization of fame attracts personalities who seek celebrity and publicity. Increased scrutiny does not scare off the egotistical, the callous, and those who want widespread public attention. Individuals who value having normal private lives for themselves and their families, or sensitive individuals with thin skins, are less likely to pursue positions of high public visibility. This effect will be harmful if the individuals who value privacy for their families are also more altruistic and considerate, or for some other reason make better leaders. One danger is that individuals who place no value on their privacy tend to seek power and control.

Greater scrutiny may discourage honest candidates more than it does dishonest candidates. Widespread media revelations of political scandals have convinced many voters that all politicians are dishonest. Any individual, no matter how honest, will come under question if placed in the public spotlight. That individual will be the subject of rumor, innuendo, slander, potential lawsuits, and speculation about his or her motives. Since even a completely honest individual cannot demonstrate absolute integrity to the public, listeners will think that the rumored charges may be true. The subsequent loss of reputation may place a greater burden on honest individuals than on dishonest individuals. If a candidate will be accused of depravity or corruption in any case, the truly honest may face an especially high loss of reputation if they enter politics.

Individuals who have already undergone extensive scrutiny—in other words, career politicians—have less to lose if they run for high office. Consequently, politics increasingly attracts the career politician. The resulting mix of candidates confirms voters' impressions that politicians are careerist or dishonest, and thus strengthens the reputational penalty faced by the honest. Politics will be full of the dishonest, although the high degree of scrutiny will check their ability to act dishonestly.[11]

For these reasons, a society with commercialized fame, and thus intense media scrutiny, does not generate great leaders. In the case of the Presidency, it produces and attracts individuals who are adept at currying public favor and avoiding public blame.

FAME VERSUS SHAME

Not only does a fame-intensive society lower the stature of moral leaders, but it changes the morality used to evaluate and regulate those leaders. A society that is rich in fame and poor in privacy tends to be poor in shame.

Fans receive constant exposure to every aspect of celebrities' lives, including their marriages, divorces, affairs, sex lives, and crimes. All forms of star behavior—both good and bad—are used to attract the attention of fans. Right and wrong are blurred and subsumed into the general category of publicity fodder.

CNN boosted its ratings by providing running coverage of the Clinton-Lewinsky scandal. Although many of the commentators condemned Clinton, they all presented the President's affair with a youthful intern as a matter for ordinary political debate and discussion. It has been treated neither as "obviously unacceptable and demanding immediate resignation" nor as "none of anybody's business." Many commentators regard either Clinton's or Kenneth Starr's behavior as shameful (or

The New Heroes and Role Models

chastise them both), but constant reiteration of these charges in fact diminishes the associated shame; the truly shameful would require but a mere mention to stifle all debate.

When newspapers and television report lots of divorces for the best-known people in society, marital failure loses its status as something shameful. Television talk shows, in their quest for audiences, outdo each other in presenting weird and sensational guests, including women who love serial killers, men who have committed incest, and spouses who have run off with the next-door neighbor. These behaviors are presented and analyzed in great detail and at length. Even when the audience does not approve, widespread discussion makes these behaviors more commonplace and less shameful and shocking.[12]

Frequent and virulent criticisms of stars further dilute the force of shame. Potential targets of local censure see that the greatest and most renowned achievers routinely are subject to enormous amounts of public condemnation. Recipients of scorn, to some extent, conclude that censure is not a real measure of unpopularity or wrongdoing, since much criticism is aimed at heroes and leaders.

For better or worse, a fame-intensive society is a morally looser society. The fame-producing technologies of modern culture—especially television—pull individuals out of their local communities and into national and international fandoms. Rather than going to the town meeting, public square, or the community pub, where much of the discussion concerns neighbors, we consume the fame of stars by staying home and watching television, or by going out to the movies. As a result, we care less about what our neighbors do. Fandom, like Albert Hirschman's concept of exit from a community, is a substitute for many kinds of local participation and voice.[13]

Can Morality Survive the Separation of Fame and Merit?

Public morality, as expressed through the famous and their stature, should not coincide with merit. Morality, like most evolved institutions, serves many functions and is pulled in many differing directions. The modern world uses public images and fame to control behavior, not to reflect merit.

Looser moral standards are part of the price we pay for constraining politicians through celebrity status and media scrutiny. Every move the President makes is scrutinized, photographed, reported, and analyzed on the evening news and in the newspapers—a far cry from the situation of the Hobbesian absolute sovereign. A celebrity politician is both a low-stature politician and a constrained and trapped politician. In essence, we sacrifice role models to limit political power.

The monitoring and visibility associated with fame serve a further end: they discourage incumbent politicians from taking large risks. The fear of negative publicity forces politicians to track public opinion rather than implement their own visions. Politicians will take risks to win office in the first place, but they typically pursue safe courses of action once in power, in order to hold onto their position.[14]

These conservative political decisions are appropriate for societies that are already on the right track. Citizens cannot discard the policies of leaders who choose risky, failed undertakings, but rather must live with the outcomes. If a President or Prime Minister makes a mistake, millions of lives and jobs may be adversely affected; in some cases the fate of countries or the entire world is at stake. Significant political risk-taking is most appropriate for societies in desperate straits (such as societies on the verge of losing wars), because they need to overcome otherwise fatal obstacles.

Note that unsuccessful risks pose fewer dangers in the arts. If Garth Brooks puts out a bad recording, the world is barely worse off, and it is even less worse off if a minor star fails to deliver a good product. The outcomes of failed projects can be discarded with few external social costs, while the good outcomes can be reproduced and distributed to wide audiences. This ability to pick and choose the successful projects raises the social benefits of artistic risk-taking. In the arts we can pick and choose from the very best of generated outcomes, but in politics we cannot. For this reason, protections against risky outcomes are especially important in the political sphere, even if the associated media scrutiny lowers the moral authority of leaders.[15]

Fame for Monopolists

The weak link between fame and moral merit results in part from largely favorable developments in moral instruction. In particular, fame is more likely to separate from merit when moral teachings are supplied in a decentralized way.

Fame typically accrues to stars who hold dominant market positions, rather than to performers with numerous close competitors. Consider the fame of businessmen. Walt Disney, Henry Ford, and Bill Gates have been three of America's most famous entrepreneurs. Each held a highly visible position in a concentrated industry—movies, automobiles, and computer operating systems, respectively. Business stars in concentrated or centralized sectors, all other things being equal, tend to become more famous than entrepreneurs in decentralized industries. Few Americans could name a famous wheat farmer, barber, or trucker, even though these professions, taken as a whole, have created great value. We have too many barbers for any single barber to be important or noteworthy. Barbering flourishes nonetheless, and indeed its widespread success, evidenced by the large numbers of barbers, holds back the fame of any single haircutter.

Morality, over time, has come more from suppliers who are decentralized like barbers and less from suppliers who are oligopolistic like automobile makers. This development does not necessarily reflect moral inequity or a practical problem. Many people draw on a wide variety of inspirational sources rather than relying on a handful of individuals to give them religious guidance. Similarly, the number of prominent charitable benefactors is larger than ever before. Our political system does not rest heavily upon the competence of any single individual, or any very small group of participants. These goods—spirituality, charity, and political leadership—are produced in increasingly decentralized fashion, and thus they generate fewer conspicuous heroes. In other words, the greater difficulty of becoming famous through moral teachings reflects the widespread distribution of morality in the modern world. Of course to some extent moral teaching has become more centralized, through preachers' use of television, for example, but to this extent moral leaders have remained famous as well.

Fame as a Brand Name

Fame often proliferates where there is uncertainty about merit, rather than where merit is high. Among its many functions, fame serves as a brand name—it gives information to fans who are otherwise unsure what to purchase or what decision to make. When in doubt, buy from a name you know. Looking to fame and to names therefore indicates underlying *doubts* about the quality of what the famous are trying to sell. This mechanism further separates fame and merit.

We do not see much fame—or brand names—in the market for ordinary house nails. Their quality, for the most part, is evident upon inspection and buyers need not resort to picking a name they know. In contrast, when fans scrutinize a compact disk, they cannot tell the quality of the music by examining the plastic container and perhaps not even by spending a few moments at a listening station. Fans rely on the name of the performer in deciding what music to buy. Names, and thus fame, play a big role in that market.[16]

The absence of fame in the nails market does not mean that home carpentry is corrupt or that the quality of nails is declining. Rather it means that we can buy good nails without thinking much about the identity of the suppliers. Similarly, the relative paucity of fame for moral preaching in part reflects that we judge moral ideas on their own terms, without worrying too much about whose name is attached to them. In cases where we are certain about what is meritorious in a given area, or can judge the merit of a product on its own terms, fame will disappear. Fame follows its economic uses, and if fame is not useful for judging moral ideas, fame in that area will dwindle.

The Practical Uses of Unfair Fame Standards

Fans apply different standards to the meritorious to induce more and better performances from them. Applying differential and unfair standards often produces better results than applying a single uniform standard, a development that again leads to a potentially beneficial separation of fame from merit.

Some stars seem to get a free ride and keep their popularity even when they behave or perform badly. Bill Clinton has been called the "Teflon President," since he endured a high degree of criticism and scandal with few reputational consequences until the Monica Lewinsky affair. Even in that matter he has survived revelations that would have downed previous Presidents. Charles Barkley has remained a popular and admired sports figure, even though he gets into bar fights and throws fans through glass windows. In other cases, fans are especially stringent; Jerry Seinfeld complained that his show was held to an excessively high critical standard once it achieved widespread popularity. When it comes to the famous, fans and critics do not apply standards of evaluation that could properly be called fair.

The application of unfair standards, however unjust it may appear, often serves fan interests, even if it separates fame from merit. Some important performers *should* face especially tough standards. A singer at Carnegie Hall faces tougher critics than a singer at a local church. Fans receive superior performances when they subject truly productive stars to greater scrutiny and criticism, at least if they do not err and set an impossibly high standard. The most important stars might appear to suffer excessive condemnation, but the tough standards force top performers to try their very best.

The criticism market, taken as a whole, acts much like price discrimination, which may be called "praise discrimination" in this context. In effect, praise-discriminating critics set higher standards for performers who crave praise dearly and for performers who can produce high-quality performances at relatively low cost. They set higher standards for the top stars. These individuals have a high demand for praise, either because they love praise more than other performers or because they can earn it more easily. Consider Placido Domingo, who has a first-rate natural voice and who loves the roar of a large crowd. Applying higher standards to Domingo makes sure he does his best, while allowing the local singer to continue in his or her

The New Heroes and Role Models

niche without fear of harsh criticism. Performers and critics group together into segmented market tiers, based partly upon the expected quality of the performance.

Splitting the market in this way helps produce more renown, but the higher-level critics must scorn the reputation of the lower-level critics if beneficial segmentation is to persist. If the low-level critics rise sufficiently in reputation, local singers will earn praise too easily for too low a price. Market segmentation will break down and praise discrimination will disappear. The efficient production of fame therefore dictates hierarchy and elitism across different parts of the market.[17]

Many stars seek to be judged by more lenient standards by feigning indifference to the opinions of critics. They rail against the critical establishment and cultivate an outsider image. In more cynical terms, these performers are trying to get a better deal for themselves. We all pretend to be uninterested when bargaining with a seller; in this case the star is bargaining with critics for praise. The more valuable the praise to stars, the more stars will pretend they do not care, in order to avoid being charged a high price for the praise. Similarly, artists may pretend that creation is a costly struggle, even when it is relatively easy, simply to receive more admiration for their outputs. The performers who crave praise the most, or who can produce at lowest cost, invest in these deceptions with special vigor. These performers otherwise would face the toughest standards from critics, given the nature of praise discrimination.

Paradoxically, performers as a whole may be worse off if they succeed in fooling critics about how much they value praise. If critics cannot classify artists into ardent praise-lovers and those who value praise only a bit, praise discrimination will become more difficult. Critics would have to apply uniform standards across the board, and standards would be too high in the local concert hall and too low in Carnegie Hall.

Note that if a given star becomes less important, perhaps because substitute performers come along, critical standards for that star *should* decline and critics *should* be inclined to offer praise more readily. As the number of comparably talented tenors rises, fans have less need of Luciano Pavarotti and they need not monitor him so closely. For this reason, we should not automatically complain when stardom becomes easier to achieve or when stars get by with lower levels of performance. The easing of critical standards reflects in part the sophistication of a society that relies less and less on dominant or irreplaceable individuals.

A second and countervailing effect causes fans to apply lower standards to irreplaceable stars. Consider fans who seek to enjoy the star's persona and status. National Basketball Association fans in Philadelphia could look only to Charles Barkley in the 1980s, because other members of the Philadelphia 76ers were unremarkable. Philadelphia fans wanted Barkley to have a high profile, to help their team, their sports culture, and their city. These fans were inclined to give Barkley a "free ride" and overlook his failings. Had the fans cast Barkley in the role of villain, they would have had nowhere else to turn. Arguably Bill Clinton has benefited from this effect as well; his defenders have seen him as the most prominent symbol of the 1960s and the Baby Boom generation.

Whether top stars are judged by tougher or looser standards, on net, depends upon which effects predominate. The critical point is that fame standards serve many functions and a reputation is more than a grade of moral merit for an individual. A reputation is part of a useful game of carrot-and-stick, imposed on stars by fans and critics. The preferred solution to this game will not necessarily link fame directly to quality of achievement.

The Evolution of Morality in a Commercial World

When commerce delinks fame and merit to any extent, merit does not disappear from social discourse or even necessarily diminish in importance as a concept. The delinkage of fame from merit may be viewed by some as negative. But it can be viewed as the liberation of merit from fame and from dependence on the famous.

Even if the fame of entertainers corrupts the realm of moral discourse, moral discourse adjusts by relying less on fame. Most people know that Eddie Murphy and Madonna are not the most virtuous individuals in society, even if their money and charisma are admired. Rather than looking to them for moral inspiration, many turn their attention elsewhere, to parents, relatives, or people renowned in realms where fame and merit are more closely linked than they are in popular culture.

Moral discourse may operate more effectively when imperfect and blemished individuals are in the public eye. Athletes, entertainers, and characters in television shows provide more complex models than do many saints, and thus they may serve as more fruitful topics of discussion.

When the meritorious and the famous are different individuals, the social vision of virtue rests less upon adulation of personalities and more on the critical analysis of personality traits. Since fans do not expect the famous to be fully moral or meritorious, they can separate the good and bad qualities of celebrities more sharply and cleanly. Fans could approve of Michael Jordan's quest for excellence in sports while disapproving of his excessive gambling. The severance of fame and merit allows us to evaluate different aspects of an individual's behavior separately, rather than judging that person as uniformly good or bad. This more cautious kind of moral discourse may be more appropriate and more realistic than the uncritical elevation of moral and political leaders as heroes and heroines. Commercialized fame, by directing fame away from moral merit, frees ideas of virtue from the cult of personality.

Heroes, by their very nature, serve as highly visible, intensified, and sharply focused reflections of various qualities, including morality. To the extent that heroes provide the relevant field for the bulk of moral discourse, morality will be excessively black and white, moral discourse will idolize some individuals undeservedly, and the conversation will conflate the evaluation of personalities with the evaluation of moral qualities. The commercialization of society improves moral discussions in some respects by shifting moral discourse out of the realm of fame.

Role models do not automatically induce moral (or immoral) behavior. Many people have already decided to act a certain way, and they seek out whichever role models will validate that behavior. Or they interpret and reinterpret the qualities of role models in ways that support their preexisting agendas. In this way as in others, fans use the famous for their own purposes.

The original nature of a role model has less influence than does the transformation of that raw material into maxims, conclusions, and interpretations through subsequent social discourse. The story of Cal Ripken, Jr., a very durable baseball player, has entered the public consciousness as a tale of heroism, even if Ripken is not a true hero by exacting moral standards. Thomas Jefferson has moved from being a virtuous Founding Father to a morally ambiguous slaveholder.

Celebrities and television figures can serve as useful subjects for moral discussion even if they are not fully virtuous or if the characters are not real. A television character, such as Ellen from the eponymous show, may prove to be a focal point for public acceptance of lesbianism. The commercialization of her identity does not detract from this function and arguably enhances it, by spreading information about her show, the sex life of her character, and her lesbian identity in real life. Many other changes in American social behavior, such as greater acceptance of premarital sex, have been promoted through situation comedies and their ability to spark broader social discussion. Fan discussions of morality exert their approbational force whether the original topic was a saint or Seinfeld.

The coordinating images—television personas—need only be highly visible; they need not have done anything real. Daniel Boorstin has complained that pseudo-events have replaced real events, but for many purposes pseudo-events are just as good or even better, if only because they can be produced and broadcast at such low cost.

The Taming of Fame

Finally, the separation of fame and merit must be viewed in historical context. Fame and merit have never been tightly connected, no matter what era we examine or whether we define merit in terms of fan preferences or some alternative moral standard. Commercialized fame, while taking relative recognition away from moral leaders, also has taken renown away from tyrants and violent rulers.

Many of the supposed "heroes" of the past were liars, frauds, and butchers to varying degrees. The association of fame with entertainers, for all its flaws, departs from earlier concepts of heroic brutality and martial virtue. Most of today's famous people have had to persuade consumers to offer their allegiance and their dollars. Nowadays fame is attained through a high-stakes game of pursuit and seduction, rather than a heroic contest or a show of force in battle. The shift in fame to entertainers is a modern extension of the Enlightenment *doux commerce* thesis that the wealth of the market civilizes morals and manners and supports an ethic of bourgeois virtue.

Cervantes was the first writer to recognize the importance of fame commercialization and the new breed of hero in commercial society. His protagonist Don Quixote seeks to create a chivalrous image that he took from the old world of medieval fame, in which knowledge of great fighting deeds was spread by word of mouth. Cervantes portrayed this ideal of martial virtue as an ironic farce. Book 2 of *Don Quixote* showed that Don Quixote does in fact attain fame, but only by virtue of being the subject of an entertaining novel. Cervantes self-consciously presented the new world of fame achieved through commercial entertainment as displacing the older world of fame achieved through chivalry and heroism.[18]

Greek mythology illustrates the depth of the connection between heroism and violence throughout Western history. One early Greek writer claimed that the goddess Hecate, as well as heroes, caused terrors, fears, and panic attacks. A fragment of Menander's work associated heroes with evil-doing rather than with benevolence. Athletes of the classical period were elevated to cult status not for their sporting achievements, but for their "deeds of violence demonstrating their wrath." Thomas Hobbes, writing many centuries later, recognized that the classic heroes were honored for their "Rapes, Thefts, and other great, but unjust, or unclean acts," including

"Adulteries . . . [and] Frauds." John Locke, in his book on education, went further when he wrote: "All the Entertainment and talk of History is of nothing almost but Fighting and Killing: And the Honour and Renown, that is bestowed on Conquerours (who for the most part are but the great Butchers of Mankind) farther mislead growing Youth, who by this means come to think Slaughter the laudable Business of Mankind, and the most Heroick of Vertues."[19]

Not surprisingly, early Christian writers were strongly opposed to fame-seeking, which they viewed as unholy. Saint Augustine wrote that the search for glory and praise at the hands of other men will lead to "open crimes." Many other Christian writers viewed fame-seeking as an impious attempt at self-aggrandizement and recommended Christian mercy as a substitute. Milton's *Paradise Lost* presents this view to a seventeenth-century English audience that had grown to expect glory-seeking and warfare as a virtuous norm.[20]

The traditions of antiquity illustrate the essentially male nature of concepts of the heroic. Heroic standards were defined largely by males, and martial virtue was exhibited primarily by men. Women (albeit imaginary ones) achieved mythological fame in their roles as goddesses, such as Aphrodite and Hera, or as mothers and wives of warriors, but they had a hard time winning fame for their independent, mortal achievements. Contemporary culture, in contrast, has erected a growing number of female icons.[21]

Princess Diana provided one example of the new feminine heroine ideal. She embodied the quality of vulnerability, and that is one reason she attracted so much interest, especially from women. Diana struck an emotional pose, spoke openly of her feelings and her failures, and admitted her problems with depression, bulimia, and her marriage. She did not hesitate to cry in public. Nor did she hide her own fascination with fame and popular culture, so different from the prevailing aloofness of British royalty. When in her twenties, Diana wanted to meet John Travolta, the star of *Saturday Night Fever*. Compare this to earlier young European rulers, who sought their place in history by conquering other nations.

The use of fame and renown to support a male-dominated vision of society runs consistently through the history of ideas. During the Renaissance and Enlightenment, critics of commercialization frequently objected to the "softness" and "effeminization" engendered by market society. Rousseau, the arch-enemy of modern civil society, feared that martial virtue would decline, and wanted to use shame and fame to re-create his ideal Spartan community. In *Letter to D'Alembert* he called for the creation of a government-run Court of Honor to be charged with approving or disapproving of individual actions whenever a suit was brought. The court would not wield coercive powers but instead would issue judgments of condemnation or praise. This court was to be especially concerned with the behavior of "all the estates in which one carries a sword, from prince to private soldier." In the same work, Rousseau criticized the portraits of virtue issued by the entertainment-driven French theater. He complained bitterly about the heroes of the playwright Racine, who were "given over to gallantry, softness, love, to everything which can effeminate man and mitigate his taste for his real duties." Unfortunately for Rousseau, the "whole French theatre breathes only tenderness; it is the great virtue to which all the others are sacrificed, or, at least, the one which is made dearest to the spectators."[22]

The New Heroes and Role Models

Today most people use the word "Spartan" as a term of disapproval or opprobrium. We consider a Spartan lifestyle to be distasteful. Two hundred years ago, most educated Englishmen and Frenchmen held the austere Greek city-state Sparta in high regard. The modern culture of entertainment has in large part driven this shift in attitudes and role models.[23]

Thomas Carlyle, writing in 1840, summarized the martial concept of the hero and the male nature of early concepts of heroism:

> We come now to the last form of Heroism; that which we call Kingship. The Commander over Men; he to whose will our wills are to be subordinated, and loyally surrender themselves, and find their welfare in doing so, may be reckoned the most important of Great Men. He is practically the summary for us of *all* the various figures of Heroism; Priest, Teacher, whatsoever of earthly or of spiritual dignity we can fancy to reside in a man, embodies itself here, to *command* over us, to furnish us with constant practical teaching, to tell us for the day and hour what we are to *do*.[24]

An anecdote from the Second World War illustrates how far the United States and the West have moved from the ideals of Carlyle. During lulls in the shooting, American GIs needled Japanese soldiers by shouting "Fuck Hirohito!" The Japanese, rather than yelling back, "Fuck Roosevelt!"—the logical riposte—instead screamed, "Fuck Babe Ruth!"—whom they regarded as a more appropriate target. The Japanese knew that Ruth, not some war hero, personified the American ideal.[25]

Ironically, the taming of fame also entails a growth in the number of violent images. Even (especially?) in a peaceful world, fans demand cathartic experiences, and fame- and profit-seeking performers respond by meeting this demand. Clint Eastwood, Bruce Lee, Arnold Schwarzenegger, and many other contemporary heroes represent the modern sublimation, transformation, and simulation of violent impulses. The same institutions that deglorify actual martial deeds—the entertainment businesses—end up glorifying images of martial deeds. In network television programming for children, each broadcast hour averages twenty-two simulations of acts of violence.[26]

Modern commercial society therefore cannot fulfill the Enlightenment promise of civilizing manners. Commercial society defangs fame and weakens the martial virtue ethic, but at the same time it provides new sources of approbation for violence. Entertaining images, to some degree, portray violence as fun and spur some individuals to perform brutal acts. The same processes that lessen the status of real violent acts make simulated violence appear more fun and more attractive.

Commercialization also induces individuals to aim their glory-seeking impulses toward peaceful ends. Rather than centralizing fame rewards in an absolutist state or repressing fame-seeking impulses, commercialization decentralizes fame into market-based niches. In highly commercial societies, fame-seekers can achieve renown in science, sports, entertainment, and many other fields. These famous individuals cannot start wars, sway elections, or exercise coercive control over the lives of other people. Contemporary stars are impotent but well-paid puppets. But these market-based heroes are meritorious in one essential way: they serve their fans rather than making their fans serve them.[27]

4   The Test of Time

In their respective eras, Il Guercino, Angelika Kauffmann, and Rosa Bonheur were thought to be among the great painters of history. Many eighteenth-century critics put Gluck, Cherubini, Cimarosa, and Gretry in the same category as Haydn and Mozart. Robert Southey was considered a major English romantic poet. Arthur Schopenhauer remarked that when we erect a monument to a man in his lifetime, we are declaring that we do not trust future generations.[1]

Other stars benefit from the test of time. Oscar Wilde died in disgrace in 1900, but today he is considered a great satirist and a suitable subject for a movie. The death of Herman Melville passed unnoticed in 1891, with *Moby-Dick* out of print. The music of Johann Sebastian Bach was not publicly performed after his death in 1750, until Felix Mendelssohn revived it in 1829. Vincent van Gogh was well regarded by Claude Monet and other cognoscenti in his lifetime, but he did not achieve a high public or critical profile until after his death. *Let Us Now*

Praise Famous Men, by James Agee and Walker Evans, fared poorly when first published but has since become a classic.[2]

The realm of long-run fame, although it overlaps with the world of short-run celebrity, operates on different principles and selects different heroes. In this chapter I ask how long-run fame is achieved. Are fame and merit more closely linked in the long run than in the short? How does fame production change as an individual shifts from the realm of celebrity into the realm of history? What biases operate in the production of long-run fame, and do these biases serve useful functions or do they corrupt our culture?

WHY WE HAVE GATEKEEPER CRITICS

Many fans want to know which Russian novels to read, which recording of Beethoven's Fifth to purchase, and which art exhibits to visit. The past offers a very large number of performers, most of whom are not appealing or interesting. Fans do not have the time and energy to sort out the good from the bad, and so they turn to specialists—gatekeeper critics—for recommendations about merit. Even if popular culture is "corrupt," markets support critics who separate high-quality from low-quality achievements.

Gatekeeper critics serve as the societal guardians of long-term renown. These well-established, conservative institutions guard entrance into canons and pantheons of achievement. Examples of gatekeeper critics include Nobel Prize committees, academic literary critics, museums, and Halls of Fame. They designate some stars as of especially high quality and promote those recommendations to fans.

Gatekeeper critics endorse performers to cement and extend their own critical reputations. If the chosen performers do well, the certifying critic will enjoy increased stature, wider influence, and augmented income. Gatekeeper critics therefore look for quality and historical importance when evaluating performers, at least relative to the emphasis favored by praise for sale. They are more likely than other critics to develop reputations for reliability and high standards because they ususaly do not exploit the mass market for immediate profit.

Academic literary critics fund their writings through their university salary, which is a function of their scholarly reputation. Museums rely on donations of money and artworks, which are attracted most easily by the most prestigious institutions. Nobel Prizes are endowed, but their influence depends on winning the respect of the scholarly community. Most Halls of Fame finance themselves through admission fees, a practice which requires that they hold a prominent position in the public eye as authoritative judges of quality. In all these cases, the desire for reputation exercises a strong or dominant influence.

Maintaining High Standards

Gatekeeper institutions use long-lived institutional structures, well-specified rules, and established customs to maintain their credibility and to ensure that they pick stars of merit. They often appoint "purist" critics, who take intrinsic pleasure in praising the best performers and enforcing high standards. These critics, motivated by conceptions of merit, induce trust in fame-generating processes. Their appointments help an institution achieve and extend gatekeeper status.

Prizes awarded by autonomous, long-lived institutions tend to be more credible than prizes awarded by nonaffiliated individuals. A prize funded and controlled by Ross Perot, for instance, would achieve little influence; Perot could not credibly signal his role as a reliable gatekeeper. Prizes handed out by a single individual may simply represent that person's idiosyncrasies, prejudices, and biases. But prizes awarded by independent, long-lived institutions reflect those institutions' willingness to invest in long-term reputation and adhere to generally accepted standards of quality.[3]

The baseball Hall of Fame in Cooperstown, New York, a typical example of a gatekeeper critic, sets out stringent induction procedures to preserve its stature over the long run. Induction is controlled by two committees, each subject to explicit rules and strong implicit conventions. The Veterans Committee, composed of former players, is limited to two selections a year, and the voting sportswriters have developed the convention of electing no more than three members in a year, except when truly exceptional players are on the ballot. From either committee a vote of 75 percent or more is required to admit a candidate.

The Hall, chartered as a nonprofit institution, is structured to satisfy a variety of constituencies and to control quality. First, the baseball Hall of Fame is operated and controlled by Clark Estates, a charitable foundation established by the Clark family in upstate New York. The administrators of Clark Estates have ultimate authority over Hall of Fame selection procedures and they have maintained high standards for the production of baseball fame. Second, the Hall is beholden to major league baseball for promotion and status. Major league baseball unofficially recognizes the authority of the Hall, but might revoke this approval if the Hall were to let standards slip. Third, the Hall of Fame depends upon the continued loyalty of its members. Members show up for induction ceremonies, help with fund-raising, and allow the Hall of Fame to market their images. Low standards would endanger the loyalty of members and thus jeopardize the Hall's effectiveness. Fourth, the Hall of Fame must keep the loyalty of its own employees and administrators. Fifth, the Hall has placed voting in the hands of the Baseball Writers Association of America, in the hope of receiving nationwide publicity in return. If the Hall ever revoked the independence of the sportswriter-voters or tried to sway them, favorable publicity would decline and might even turn negative. Finally, the Hall must appeal to the 400,000 visitors who come each year and pay attendance fees. All of these constituencies encourage the Hall to protect the value of its franchise.[4]

The Hall has been largely successful in maintaining standards. The baseball expert Bill James conducted a detailed study to ascertain which players have been awarded or denied admission unjustly. Although he came up with some examples of bad decisions (Phil Rizzuto should not belong, Jim Kaat should), for the most part his statistical analysis confirmed the evaluations made by the Hall. Most players in the Hall of Fame were in fact the best players of their time. Furthermore, standards have risen rather than declined. In percentage terms, the number of baseball players who earn admission into the Hall has remained constant or fallen.[5]

Many reputation-producing institutions, such as Halls of Fame and the bodies that award prizes, organize as nonprofits to signal that their endorsements are not for sale. A for-profit might sell its Nobel Prize in Economic Science to Bill Gates, whereas a nonprofit would be more likely to choose a recipient with higher academic status. The individual who would pay the most for the prize would not necessarily give the prize highest status. The prizes of highest status therefore are awarded either by nonprofit charitable foundations or by governments, both of which lack a well-defined profit motive. The academic members of the Nobel Prize committee care about their long-term reputations and thus have strong incentives to pick accomplished individuals as prize recipients. The structure of the Nobel institution prevents committees from accepting money from a would-be buyer of the prize, or bribes from someone desiring to influence the choice of recipient.

Note that not-for-profit criticism may come from for-profit sources of funding. The literary Booker Prize, which is funded by a British agricultural corporation, is administered by an independent trust. Some for-profit parent companies forbid their critics to take bribes, to ensure the credibility of the evaluations they produce. The Michelin restaurant guides are produced by a for-profit parent company, but Michelin requires its guides to rate restaurants objectively and by very high standards. Fewer fans would buy the Michelin guides if it were known that the critics took bribes from chefs, so Michelin employs strict and conservative evaluators.[6]

Some critics demonstrate their trustworthiness and market their name by limiting the fineness of the gradations they award. The Michelin guides give top restaurants one star, two stars, or three stars, rather than using a more finely grained standard, such as a scale from 1 to 100. *The Penguin Guide to Classical Recordings* awards CDs one star, two stars, or three stars. Some critics, such as the movie commentators Gene Siskel and Roger Ebert, have employed a binary system of "thumbs up" or "thumbs down."

Critics choose grosser scales for at least three reasons. First, such evaluations are easier to remember and therefore easier to talk about. I can remember that a Michelin restaurant is a "one-star," but not that the same establishment earned a 16.5 on the scale used by the Gault-Milleau guides. Second, these "bottom-line" evaluations cannot be misunderstood or distorted by selective quotation. Third, the grosser scale makes overvaluations relatively easy to recognize and helps precommit the critic to high standards. By choosing the grosser rankings, Michelin puts more of its credibility on the line if it makes a mistake in evaluation. The relatively gross scale implies that any mistake will be a significant and noticeable one. The Gault-Milleau books, which appeal to more casual eaters, use a 1 to 20 scale (supplemented by lengthy verbal evaluations), whereas Michelin appeals to the gourmet, holds higher standards, and uses a grosser scale.[7]

Not Just Fifteen Minutes of Fame

Gatekeeper critics belie Andy Warhol's claim that everyone will be famous for only fifteen minutes. Warhol correctly identified one aspect of the fame market, the rocket-like rise to celebrity, but he misread the larger trend. Gatekeeper critics, such as Halls of Fame, deal largely in long-term recognition. They look to their own long-run reputation and to maintaining the long-run reputations of the performers they endorse. Warhol did not recognize that short-term celebrity and long-run fame are largely complements rather than substitutes. The modern proliferation of Halls of Fame, prizes, awards, and academic canons is financed by the same wealthy, commercial societies that produce movie stars and famous athletes.

Modern technologies and market entrepreneurship have made fame more durable than ever before. We have better access to the works of Mozart and Shakespeare than fans of earlier eras. More people saw Wagner's Ring cycle on public television in 1990 than had seen it live in all Ring productions since the 1876 premiere. Recorded boxed sets and complete editions of little-known composers are now widely available. Published catalogs with color plates bring the works of painters and sculptors to larger audiences. Videocassette stores, video laser disks, and cable television spread the fame of movie stars and directors from previous generations.[8]

Warhol's own reputation has proved durable to date. There is an entire art museum, in Pittsburgh, devoted to his works and bearing his name. His small Chairman Mao paintings, relatively minor works in his canon, sold for $6,000 in 1987 but now sell for six-figure sums. Nonprofit museums, acting in conjunction with for-profit auction houses, will keep Warhol's name and works in front of the public eye for a long time. In the eighteenth century Jonathan Swift voiced a view similar to Warhol's in the satirical poem "Verses on the Death of Dr. Swift". Swift suggested that he would be forgotten a year after his death and replaced in the public mind by newer writers. Yet Swift, like Warhol, will be promoted by gatekeeper critics for centuries. Both nonprofit literary critics and for-profit bookstores maintain Swift's reputation and promote his written works.[9]

CYCLES OF FAME

The traditional treatment of why the famous and their creations stand the test of time focuses on the clarification of our critical sense as we accumulate listening time and reading time and engage in or listen to aesthetic debate. But long-run fame is governed by economic principles as well. The reputation of a star undergoes a cycle, determined by changes in the relative influence of praise for sale and gatekeeper critics.

When new performers hit the market, they tend to rely heavily on advertising and praise for sale, as I discussed in

Chapter 2. To the extent that those promotional tactics succeed in linking the performer to a constituency of fans, the performer will become known and achieve celebrity. Praise for sale mobilizes fan support to produce short-run fame.

The long-run reputations of new performers nonetheless will remain unsettled. Huge sums of money are at stake in the critical dialogue about celebrity. Publicists are paid to praise new products, blurring the difference between criticism and advertising. Even if no single critic "sells out," promoters give favorable opinions for new products more publicity than unfavorable opinions. Top critics disparage the works of John Grisham, but the publisher nonetheless can find and distribute some words of praise or use marketing power to solicit favorable blurbs. Fans, who often do not know how seriously to take this praise, will be confused about the true merits of new products. No gatekeeper critic will intervene to offer a more final or authoritative judgment, at least not in a manner that is decisive in the court of public opinion. Uncertainty will reign about the author's merit, however we choose to define that notion.

As a performer passes into history and leaves popular discourse, he or she falls increasingly outside the range of advertising and praise for sale. It is easier for intermediaries to make money from new performers than from old ones. The 1997–98 receipts for *Titanic* far exceed those for *Gone with the Wind,* even though the latter was rereleased in theaters at that time. Most bestselling books, CDs, and movies are recent products rather than reissues. Television reruns are common, but the most highly rated shows are new productions. We do not see billboards for John Keats. For this reason, short-term celebrity is based on commercial factors far more than is long-term fame.

As the importance of immediate publicity declines, gatekeeper critics will begin to wield more influence over an individual's or a work's reputation. Older performers and products will move into realms where they compete for long-run fame. Gatekeeper critics will examine the merits of these performers and issue their evaluations accordingly. The artist or performer will have a chance of entering a canon, being inducted into a Hall of Fame, winning a Nobel Prize, or receiving some other designation of long-run historical import. According to one estimate, the average age of a Hall of Fame inductee is 66.37 years.[10]

If the noncommercial opinions of gatekeeper critics are aesthetically superior to praise for sale, criticism will be of relatively high quality for unprofitable and declining genres, and will be of lower quality for profitable genres on the rise. The declining genres will be relatively free of commercial promotion, and as a result, truth will become more evident. Literary critics who survey nineteenth-century poetry are not influenced much by the prospect of payola. They serve as gatekeepers and they recommend William Blake and William Wordsworth to readers on grounds of merit. Much of the puffery about the Spice Girls, in contrast, is written by paid publicists.

The common perception will develop that newer artistic genres are of lower quality than older ones. Capitalism, which is preoccupied with innovation, makes new products extremely visible. Yet publicity and criticism about such products will be the most "corrupt." The most visible cultural products are the most difficult to evaluate on the basis of merit because of the predominance of praise for sale and the paucity of definitive gatekeeper opinions available for their evaluation. We will never understand the commercial culture of the present as well as the now decommercialized culture of the past.[11]

As time goes on, we process the past with increasing speed. As a society becomes wealthier, supports more critics, and has more channels of communication, the competition to establish historical canons intensifies. Giorgio Vasari established the canon for Florentine art more than a hundred years after many of its leading creators had died. Masaccio, Donatello, and Masolino, not to mention Giotto, were but distant memories in Vasari's time—Donatello died in 1466 and the first edition of Vasari's *Lives* appeared in 1550. In the intervening eighty-four years, no comparable critic was assessing those artists. By contrast, Pop Art and Abstract Expressionism, neither very old, have already generated a massive critical discourse in magazines and books. The artistic canon for the 1960s will continue to change, but we already have a provisional canon consisting of Andy Warhol, Jasper Johns, and Roy Lichtenstein, among others. Similarly, "classic rock" has become a well-established field that includes Bob Dylan, the Rolling Stones, and the Beatles with relatively little dissent.

THE BIASES OF GATEKEEPER CRITICS

Gatekeeper critics do not separate fame from merit in the same way that praise for sale does. The ten writers with the most academic citations in English are (in order) Shakespeare, Joyce, Goethe, Chaucer, Milton, Dante, Faulkner, James, Dickens, and T. S. Eliot. We may or may not agree that these are the ten best authors ever, but surely the long-run fame-generating process does not favor individuals with new products, as does praise for sale.[12]

Gatekeeper critics nonetheless fail to serve as absolute guardians of merit. Even the guardians of long-run fame find their behavior shaped by economic constraints and opportunities.

Gatekeeper critics are not typically cynical maximizers of profit, but if they cannot replenish their finances they eventually will cease to exist. Several biases therefore influence the distribution of long-run fame. In this context I define bias as relative to the preferences of informed experts—relative to the preferences of the gatekeeper critics themselves. Bias exists if gatekeeper critics, operating under real-world constraints, produce rankings that would deviate from the results of an honest and well-informed debate about performer merits.

To the extent that gatekeeper critics are funded and controlled by elites, they tend to overrepresent the preferences of those elites in their evaluations. Witness the well-known multiculturalist charge that there are too many "dead white males" in historical canons. Even if "white male elites" do not deliberately downplay the role of women and minorities in history, they may simply fail to see the relevant contributions of other groups. Many critics from older generations have had an easier time understanding the music of Mozart than that of Muddy Waters, and therefore they do more to promote the fame of Mozart. Similarly, for a long time white male critics favored the paintings of Diego Rivera over those of his wife, Frida Kahlo. Her uniquely female perspective escaped the attention of many art critics for decades, although in recent times her reputation has matched and arguably eclipsed her husband's. Conservatives charge that today a new elite—academic left-wing multiculturalists—excessively promotes the reputations of its favored stars.

Critics use their discretionary powers to shape opinion for their own benefit. Gatekeepers reap rewards to the extent that they are considered guardians of quality, but they help produce the very perceptions used to evaluate them. We approve of the Louvre because it displays art by Leonardo and Rubens, but also we approve of Leonardo and Rubens because their paintings hang in the Louvre. Gatekeeper critics advance some performers over others, knowing that their promotions will be self-validating to some extent.

The market power of many gatekeeper institutions supports their ability to shape the fame agenda. Business firms come and go, but the list of top prizes and awards has not changed much. The Michelin guides, the Nobel Prizes, the Academy Awards, and the baseball Hall of Fame have been opinion leaders for many decades and hold relatively secure positions for the future. The second most prestigious arbiter of past baseball excellence, whatever or whoever it may be, will have low stature relative to the most prestigious.[13]

Gatekeeper critics tend to favor stars with highly durable outputs and achievements. Mimes may gain renown in their lifetime, but their chances of achieving long-run fame are relatively slight because live performances are very important in their genre. Jazz improvisors, stars of modern dance, and brilliant orators have similar problems in perpetuating their reputations. In contrast, the outputs of John Wayne, Pink Floyd, and Leo Tolstoy will not disappear or deteriorate with the passage of time.

For related reasons, stars who produce impressive statistics, or other definitive measures of achievement, will fare especially well over time. Gatekeeper critics can endorse such stars without fear of being criticized or second-guessed. Buck Ewing, who played baseball early in the twentieth century, was in his own time considered the equal of Ty Cobb, Honus Wagner, and Babe Ruth. Yet Ewing's career statistics, although admirable, do not overwhelm the modern observer. Ewing was inducted into the Hall of Fame in 1939, but his name is familiar only to the keenest of present-day baseball fans. The more time has elapsed, the greater the part measurable feats play in determining fame.[14]

Gatekeeper critics do not completely avoid the biases of advertising and praise for sale, as I discussed in Chapter 2. All gatekeeper critics are tempted at the margin by market opportunities. University presses now take greater care to publish and promote authors whose works will sell, rather than authors of lengthy tomes about medieval history. To an increasing degree, universities are requiring that their presses turn a profit or at least cover their costs. Recently, also, art museums have begun selling Monet T-shirts, greeting cards, and coffee mugs. At the same time, purely commercial enterprises are intruding into the gatekeepers' realm. Paintings by Vincent van Gogh now serve as inspiration for images on sweaters, French desserts, T-shirts, and a "Great Artists Series" Barbie Doll, dressed in a sunflower. A dentist in France paints van Gogh reproductions on the front teeth of clients.[15]

In addition, gatekeeper critics cannot help noticing the commercial promotions that surround them. Praise for sale can accelerate the speed with which a star, such as Norman Mailer, is brought to the attention of the gatekeepers. If a performer with some degree of intellectual plausibility achieves widespread celebrity, gatekeeper critics will be more likely to consider the merits of that star. Even if gatekeeper critics snobbishly hold popular success against the star, they cannot help wondering whether the star is any good, preparing the way for reevaluation later on.

Contrary to the usual trend, the reputations of some creators move from the realm of historical fame back into commercialized promotions. When entrepreneurs discover that old works can be packaged in new ways, praise for sale reenters

           The Test of Time

the picture. The British Bloomsbury group—Virginia Woolf, E. M. Forster, Lytton Strachey, Roger Fry, Duncan Grant, Vanessa Bell, John Maynard Keynes, to name the most famous members—has grown in fame over the last thirty years, but not primarily for scholarly reasons. Starting in the 1960s, the group became a mass market attraction for the educated lay audience in the United Kingdom and the United States. A stream of movies and books have brought group members before the public eye. The movie *Carrington* dealt with the life of Strachey, while *Orlando* put one of Virginia Woolf's works on the screen. These popularizations also feed back into the scholarly world, by stimulating the interest of graduate students in the Bloomsbury group and their creations.[16]

In the case of Shakespeare, his short-run celebrity and long-run fame have risen together. Shakespeare died in 1616, but his works continue to inspire new creations, both on the stage and in the cinema and television. Baz Luhrmann has produced a rap version of *Romeo and Juliet*, drawing upon Haitian Voodoo art for its visuals and set in contemporary Miami. Apparently without irony, the 1996 movie was entitled *William Shakespeare's Romeo and Juliet*. When older works leave the exclusive hands of gatekeeper critics and reemerge into contemporary commercial culture, we have a central component of the postmodern.[17]

As well as being affected by the biases already discussed, many gatekeeper critics display a pronounced conservative bent. Since many fans (and performers) cannot easily distinguish between an innovation and a lowering of standards, reputation-conscious gatekeeper critics limit their innovations. Institutions that produce long-run fame become hard to influence and hard to change. Their organizational structures become more rigid and more tightly knit; they apply checks and balances to decision-making procedures; and they give conservative critics great control over award selections. Long-lived gatekeeper institutions have time-honored rules and procedures for the allocation of fame.

The use of nonprofit institutions for selecting winners of prizes and awards further supports conservatism of evaluation. Nonprofit gatekeepers, when they are safe from pecuniary corruption, do not respond to changing market conditions with the speed or efficiency of for-profit corporations. Halls of Fame and prize committees tend to adhere closely to standard operating procedures and to rely heavily on tradition. Since nonprofits have no incentive to make money, they are less likely than for-profits to undergo the dynamic internal restructuring or radical change that often accompanies the quest for greater profit. The same mechanism that preserves standards—insulation from the profit motive—also limits innovation.

To credibly demonstrate their high standards, gatekeeper critics must show that they are not swept up in current fads and that they value the time-honored achievements of the past. These critics try to signal their soundness by praising the established stars of previous eras. Gatekeeper critics therefore produce an image of long-term reliability by promoting themselves as "cultural pessimists." They glorify the past unduly in an attempt to establish conservative credentials and establish credibility with their audiences.

The dead and the retired come in for special praise, in part because they possess no further capacity to embarrass or disappoint the critics. James Dean and Jim Morrison, who died young, probably attained greater fame thereby than they would had they lived longer. Dean probably would have made a string of bad and embarrassing movies and Morrison's musical career could only have gone downhill. Both would have lost their image as "cool" had they survived. John F. Kennedy, had he not been assassinated, might have ended up largely forgotten, like Jimmy Carter, rather than as a symbol of American heroism and leadership. Once people are safely dead, critics can offer homage without fear of being dishonored in return. Praising the dead identifies the critic with a reliable standard more effectively than does praising the unpredictable living.[18]

When fans complain about the conservatism of gatekeeper critics, they have a valid point, even when they continue to consult those same critics. From the point of view of the fans, the (unattainable) best outcome involves critics who are both reliable and innovative. But critics, who want to demonstrate their trustworthiness, can show reliability only by sacrificing some innovation. Fans end up with commentary that is more conservative than they would ideally desire.

The ability of gatekeeper critics to certify performers and enhance reputations gives them discretionary powers and can lead to discrimination and favoritism. Gatekeeper critics face excess demand for their free endorsements, at least in the absence of payola. When a critic can pick and choose which performer to endorse, that critic can discriminate at very low or no cost. Critics in this position will tend to recommend friends of the family, performers who share the same political outlook, or performers who satisfy their own tastes. Inside connections will prove important for procuring stardom, especially at the entry level, where critical endorsements have the greatest value.[19]

THE MATTHEW EFFECT

Gatekeeper critics often endorse established performers to support their own reputations and security. Academic citation practices reflect this tendency in pronounced form. Once a scientist starts being commonly cited for a contribution, that scientist continues to be cited. It is then hard for any other scientist to achieve recognition for the same contribution, even if that scientist deserves equal credit. In short, citations beget citations, a dramatic demonstration of the "Matthew effect," a term derived from a phrase in the book of Matthew: "Unto every one that hath shall be given and he shall have abundance.[20]

The reasons for conservative citation practices are clear. When one scientist cites the work of another, the likelihood of praise innovation is small. A scientist cannot achieve much glory by having been the first to cite a notable work, but citing an unreliable work may decrease the scientist's credibility. Scientists receive fame for the quality of their research rather than for the quality of their citations; risky citation practices have a downside but little upside. Scientists therefore behave as conservative gatekeepers when it comes to citations.[21]

In Arthur Schopenhauer's view, people supply praise only when it contributes to their own glory. People praise to promote their own reputations, not to honor the person being praised. Most typically, they praise to demonstrate the superiority their own taste. Praisers, Schopenhauer wrote, "act in the spirit of Xenophon's remark: he must be a wise man who knows what is wise." Many people praise Shakespeare not in an act of real homage but to display their own wisdom and demonstrate their excellent literary taste, hoping to capture a share of Shakespeare's renown. Once the value of a work or individual has been widely recognized, individuals will compete to praise and honor it. According to Schopenhauer, the famous find it easy to get attention, and people who are not already famous find it difficult to achieve renown; they meet censure more often than praise.[22]

The Test of Time

Praise from a given critic, for a given performer, tends to hold steady or rise over time, even more than the persistence of talent and taste would dictate. Once an academic advisor helps his or her student get a teaching position, that same advisor will be inclined to write a letter supporting the former student's bid for tenure. Once fans have sung the praises of a new rock star to their friends, they are less inclined to complain if subsequent albums and CDs are lower in quality. Critics who have praised a performer have some stake in the subsequent success of that person. The performer's success will make the critic look good, whereas failure will make the critic look less reliable. Famous performers have induced a large number of critics to have a reputational stake in their status, thus supporting a conservative inertia of praise in their favor.[23]

Well-known writers do not receive comparable attention from publishers when they submit manuscripts under pseudonyms; Doris Lessing tried such a strategy and failed. One young author retyped and submitted Jerzy Kosinski's *Steps* under his own name to fifteen publishers and fifteen agents. At the time, *Steps* had sold more than 400,000 copies and had received the National Book Award for 1969. All of the publishers and agents rejected the manuscript because they were unwilling to take a chance on an unknown writer.[24]

The Matthew effect, however, is by no means a universal phenomenon. Many settings offer strong incentives for innovative assignments of fame and credit. The field of biography, for instance, encourages critical innovation more than does scientific citation. Early biographers of Darwin, Freud, Einstein and other geniuses stood some chance of achieving fame in their own right—the Freud biography by Ernest Jones is still renowned, for instance. Biographers therefore compete to discover neglected historical figures who are nonetheless interesting and fame-worthy. Unlike researchers choosing which scientist to cite, biographers can internalize some of the gains from entrepreneurial risk-taking if they unearth a new and interesting subject to write about or discover a new angle on a familiar subject.

If a literary critic discovers a great writer before anyone else does, the critic may establish his or her own reputation by being the first to recognize that individual's work. The critic may write a biography or study of the writer, may track down and publish the writer's letters, may gain special expertise in a given area, and so on. Just as a performer often reaps special rewards for being the first important creator in a given area, so a critic may get special rewards for being the first insightful evaluator in an area. Rather than conforming to the evaluations of others, praise entrepreneurs compete to discover new talent

Praising Shakespeare may establish a critic's reputation as sound or reliable, but it hardly creates an impression of profound judgment. To exceed the reputations of competitors and to establish a valuable market foothold, a critic must take some chances. Praising Pramoedya Toer, a modern Indonesian writer, as a genius offers higher upside potential than praising Shakespeare, at least in the long run, once Toer's reputation rises to its deserved level.

Critics tend to take more risks and produce more entrepreneurial praise when they enjoy little surplus, relative to their alternative occupations. Young writers for rap music fanzines have little to lose if they are fired, given their low or zero wage. For this reason, they tend to eschew praise conformity and take critical risks. Even at *Source,* one of the more established rap publications, the average age of the members of the editorial staff is twenty-five, and each is either black or Hispanic. By contrast, older critics with valuable sinecures and perks tend to act more conservatively, to preserve and extend the value of their critical franchise.[25]

For similar reasons, critics with highly specialized talents tend to be more conservative. Critics with more general talents have greater alternative opportunities and are more inclined to take chances and act entrepreneurially. As a genre develops, and the need for specialized critical training becomes more intense, processes of evaluation tend to become more conservative. Risky and innovative criticism relies on the continuing arrival of new market entrants with low perks, little to lose, and high propensities to take risk.

The use of large corporate structures to evaluate writers, musicians, and other performers frequently discourages innovation. The larger the corporation, the greater the likelihood that the manager enjoys relative autonomy from the shareholders. The manager will build an empire of perks and personal relationships, and will seek to protect his job against the possibility of dismissal. Perk-besotted managers want to play it safe. If that same manager serves as a critic of talent, the desire for comfort and safety will translate into relatively conservative evaluations of talent. The manager will incur large losses if he makes a mistake—he could even be fired—but will not reap all of the benefits from succeeding in a gamble. That is one reason why so much of the innovation in modern popular music has come from the "independent" record companies, rather than from the established majors.

In smaller firms, the interests of the critic are more closely aligned with the interests of the shareholders. Consider a one-person firm where the same person is owner and critic; that person will benefit greatly from successful gambles and thus has strong incentives to take chances. Motown was highly innovative when it was owned and run by Berry Gordy, but eventually it was sold to outside investors, lost its special flair, and entered the musical mainstream.

Many successful innovator critics evolve into older, more conservative institutions and move into the tier of gatekeeper critics. If an innovator critic consistently picks future market winners, fans will continue to look to that critic. In the 1960s, the magazine *Rolling Stone* led the way in praising and recommending rock and roll, and was initially considered an innovative and radical upstart. *Rolling Stone* is now at the center of mainstream thought on contemporary popular music; its periodic features on "the greatest rock albums ever" have considerable authority. The magazine is an effective codifier of past achievements, but it is rarely in the vanguard when it comes to discovering new talent.

Criticism as a whole need not become more conservative since new critics are constantly entering the arena. Yet the sources of new and innovative critical ideas do shift over time. Originally successful and innovative sources of criticism tend to ossify, eventually being upstaged in creativity by up-and-coming parvenus.

THE INFLATION PROBLEM

The reputations of awards, like the reputations of performers, face the test of time, and the passage of time does not always favor merit. Montaigne observed that "honor is a privilege that derives its principal essence from rarity." Yet valuable awards, prizes, and honors become commonplace if they are handed out with insufficient discrimination. Fame inflation separates fame from merit by debasing the value of once-honorable designations.[26]

The U.S. government awards military medals more indiscriminately than ever before. In the Revolutionary War, only three Purple Hearts were awarded. In the Battle of Iwo Jima, in World War II, casualties totaled 28,686 (6,821 dead). Every one of these casualties received a Purple Heart. In 1989 a paratrooper received a Purple Heart simply because he had suffered heatstroke during the invasion of Panama.[27]

The inflation of American medal-giving escalated dramatically during the Vietnam War. By February 1971, 1,273,987 medals for Vietnam bravery had been awarded, as compared to 50,258 for the Korean War and 1,766,546 for all of World War II. By 1969 fifty-six generals had returned from Vietnam, and twenty-six had received awards for valor, even though only one general had died from enemy fire at that time. After the American military action in Grenada, 8,612 medals were handed out, even though only 7,200 troops landed. Only 19 were killed and 116 wounded. Some of the medal recipients never saw active combat or left the United States. Everyone in the military received an award for the Gulf War, and the army now has created a special medal for the completion of boot camp. The navy awarded combat ribbons to the crew of the *Vincennes* for their action in mistakenly shooting down an Iranian civilian jet in 1988.[28]

The Catholic church has been inflating away the value of sainthood. From 1642 until recently, the Catholic church enforced rigorous standards for its sainthood awards. Procedures for canonizing involved strict rules and could take centuries. The church had ruled that the Congregation for the Causes of Saints must wait at least five years after a person's death to consider a petition for sainthood. A "postulator" was then appointed to look into the matter. Writings would be collected, a biography would be written, tribunals would be held, and votes would be taken. After some time the pope could declare the candidate "Blessed," thus conferring the intermediate distinction of beatification. But even after that, evidence of further miracles was required for sainthood, and it could take centuries to assemble sufficient evidence. The canonization of France's immensely popular Saint Thérèse of Lisieux twenty-eight years after her death, in 1897, set a speed record for the time.

Today canonization comes more rapidly and more indiscriminately. Now only one miracle is required for sainthood instead of two. The office of Devil's Advocate (*sic*), which takes an adversarial role in the canonization process, has lost its power. As of 1995, Pope John Paul II had canonized 276 saints and beatified 768 people; the previous record had been held by Pius XII, who beatified 23 people and canonized 33 saints. John Paul II has canonized more people than all other popes in this century combined. He has sought to increase the popularity of the church, even if this means diminishing the value of the honors held by earlier saints. He has been most liberal with canonization in third world areas, such as Vietnam and Africa, where the church has the best chance of growing rapidly. Media attention also plays a role. The death of Mother Teresa in 1997 was followed immediately by speculation about the possibilities for her rapid or accelerated canonization.[29]

WHEN IS FAME DEBASEMENT LIKELY?

Fame inflation is common, but it is most likely where its cost is lowest. When critics certify quality for fans and consumers, as do gatekeeper critics, debasement is improbable. Reputation-conscious gatekeeper critics will lose reputation, income, and perks if they inflate away the value of the fame they award. But they will receive more attention and prestige if they ensure that every selection is noteworthy. These critics thus support merit by protecting and extending the value of their awards.

Debasement is more frequent when its corresponding benefits are high relative to its costs. Some critics are less concerned with certifying quality than with eliciting as much output from performers as possible. I call these critics motivator critics. Compared to gatekeeper critics, these critics give less thought to merit and are quicker to debase fame. Once the earlier awards have been used to elicit some output, these critics are tempted to issue more awards to draw forth even more output.

The military is a motivator critic to a large extent. Its immediate goal is to win the current or next war, rather than to certify the merit of award-winning soldiers. The military therefore increases the quantity of medals to elicit more support for fighting, without caring greatly that past awards no longer serve valuable certification functions. The average U.S. citizen or member of Congress, when deciding how much political support to offer the military, does not look closely at the average quality of Purple Heart awards, and people do not use military honors to judge the quality of their next-door neighbors.[30]

Motivator critics drive fame inflation in the Catholic church in a similar manner. Church members no longer use the rubric of sainthood to evaluate the merit of past religious figures. Instead, sainthood has become a marketing device to generate publicity for the church and to attract new members. The church itself, at least, benefits from this inflation. Church membership is rising in many parts of the developing world, while the lower prestige attributed to earlier, now-dead saints does not entail significant costs.

The Tragedy of the Verbal Commons

Critics protect standards and designations of merit only when they have a reputational stake in the meaning of a given award. The Nobel Prize committee cares what the phrase "Nobel quality scientist" means; their institutional rewards depend on the quality of their brand name.

In many evaluation processes, however, no trademark, brand name, private institution, or copyrightable asset is involved. For instance, when the award is a verbal designation, such as "great," no single critic has much stake in the meaning of that word. The meaning of the word thus tends to deteriorate over the long run. Will Rogers told the story of a customer who went to the drugstore for toothpaste and asked for a small tube. The druggist handed him a large tube, and the customer complained, saying "I wanted small." The druggist responded: "Mister, I've got family-size or economy-size or large. But large is the smallest I got."[31]

In the language of property rights economics, the meanings of words form a "common pool," which users will deplete with little or no regard for the future. The phrase "Tragedy of the Commons" has been used to refer to depletion of this kind. When no single speaker gains from preserving a given standard, the standard tends to erode. Over time the collective meaning of the message weakens, given the slight (or perhaps not so slight) alteration introduced by each individual speaker.

When listeners hear a new pop star praised as "fantastic" or "awesome," they do not know if she is merely good or if she is truly a once-in-a-lifetime wonder. When a real wonder does come along, it is difficult to credibly demonstrate her abilities with superlatives alone. Language tends to communicate some kinds of information less effectively over time because of the common pool problem. General words and constructions of praise tend to lose meaning and become separated from merit.

Market Responses to Verbal Debasement

Critics often protect their speech from debasement by privatizing it, by developing proprietary standards. The Michelin company has protected its "Michelin stars" by trademarking the Michelin name. It has good reason to preserve the value of its standard, since the profits of Michelin come from its reputation for reliability. Customers to buy the Michelin books because of the accuracy of the recommendations they contain. Modern fans have access to a wide variety of such private standards, including Pulitzer Prizes, Leonard Maltin's published movie rankings, and selections of Halls of Fame, to name just a few examples of many. All of these standards have copyright or trademark protection and therefore are owned by some institution or individual.

Credible outside commentators can usefully make reference to the Michelin standard. Rather than telling my friend Randall Kroszner that a restaurant is "great" or "excellent," I tell him it is "Michelin one-star quality." Then Randy knows what I mean. Speakers use Michelin standards as benchmarks for comparison, even if Michelin does not rate the restaurant in question. The phrase "Michelin one-star quality" has a generally understood and well-defined meaning, while the word "wonderful" does not.[32]

When they refer to a trademark, speakers are using relative comparisons to communicate information. Relative comparisons, rather than quantities of effusion, check praise inflation. When a soprano is lauded as "the best since Maria Callas," fans can pinpoint the claimed level of quality with some degree of accuracy. As "wonderful" loses its meaning, sincere critics use fixed benchmarks and comparisons with greater frequency. We see the same means used to preserve standards in letters of recommendation. Professors who write letters now provide direct comparisons with increasing frequency. Professors who write that a student is "very good" are ignored, whereas professors who write that the student is "the best in the class" have some influence. The comparison makes a claim that cannot credibly by made for all other candidates and thus has greater credibility.

PRIVATIZATION AND THE LANGUAGE PURISTS

The so-called language purists, such as William Safire, misunderstand the evolution of language when they decry the decline of English over time. The English language shows privatization rather than general decline or corruption. The public sphere of English has indeed lost meaning, as the language purists suggest, but the privatized sphere of the language produces more meaning and information than ever before. Today's writers and speakers may not have the grammar, style, and eloquence of times past, but private standards, company brand names, product names, and private definitions of quality—such as the Michelin stars—all produce far greater value today than ever before.[33]

The Test of Time

Private standards and trademarks limit the costs of merit erosion in the public sphere of language. The inflation of meaning for the word "wonderful" has not led to significant costs. If speakers had no other means of expressing the concept in a given context, some private firm would find it profitable to come along and define a relevant standard. Indeed, in the context of restaurants, the phrase "Michelin three-star" provides the required information, and can be translated to mean "truly wonderful," without erosion or inflation. As a result, the meaningful part of a language, at least in a market economy, becomes more commercial.

Although the United States has a relatively degenerate level of public speech, its commercialism provides an extraordinarily wide realm of private symbols, standards, trademarks, and so on, all of which express meaning. In these regards the English language has never been richer. Speakers can use privatized or nonprivatized media, as their purposes dictate. Individual speakers who want to avoid exaggeration can resort to private standards to convey more precise comparisons.

As linguistic meaning shifts into privatized areas, fame follows. The existence of Michelin standards makes it easier and more meaningful for chefs to win fame for their performances. The existence of Academy Awards makes it easier for actors and actresses to cement their long-run reputations.

Praise for moral leaders cannot draw upon privatized standards with the same ease as praise for chefs. Commerce and praise for sale define standards of excellence for goods that are bought and sold (music, movies, food, clothes) rather than for goods that are acquired for free, such as preaching. We thus find another reason why fame for actors and other entertainers increases relative to fame for moral leaders. Commercialization provides better and more accurate standards for evaluating and discussing entertainers and other commercial figures than for assessing preachers. Profit-seeking—this time working through the creation of private standards of value—again both mobilizes and distorts the production of renown.

5   The Proliferation of Fame

The modern world generates fame without requiring consensus on which performers are most meritorious. The decentralization of our market economy allows production—including the production of fame—to proceed without an overall plan. As honors, prizes, and reputations proliferate, they necessarily become separated from merit. Indeed, as markets distribute fame more widely and more diversely, most fame rewards will stand apart not only from merit but from *any* particular standard.

IS FAME A SUPERSTARS MARKET?

The "superstars" model developed by Sherwin Rosen implies that fame becomes more concentrated over time, at least in sectors with reproducible products and performances. Reproducibility supposedly allows one individual, or a small number of individuals, to dominate the market. Why listen to the second-best pop star, or a mediocre local singer, when the best is available on a compact disk? As technology makes reproducibility easier, the demand for the best supposedly becomes stronger. Michael Jackson, by making compact disks, suppos-edly takes away the market for the local nightclub singer. Robert H. Frank and Philip J. Cook, in *The Winner-Take-All Society*, stress that "winner-take-all markets have expanded and intensified."[1]

The superstars model suggests that we face an ongoing decline in the diversity of our culture. If all performers shoot for the superstar position, they will pursue the most popular styles at the expense of minority tastes. Furthermore, fame-seeking will become a negative-sum game, since only one star can achieve the top position in the market. Too many people will seek fame, but too few will achieve it. Frank and Cook sug-gest using tax policy to restrict fame-seeking in the interests of equality and economic growth.[2]

In my more optimistic view, the superstars phenomenon is weakening rather than intensifying. The superstars model focuses excessively on a single mechanism and neglects coun-tervailing forces that favor diversity. Fame is a positive-sum game, not a negative-sum one, as is often suggested. Given the benefits of trading praise for performance, markets continually find new means of accommodating and attracting more fame-seeking.

The music market illustrates how reproducibility can sup-port a variety of tastes and the decentralization of rewards. Lesser-known performers, such as John Cage, Sun Ra, and Lee Perry, have used recordings to sell to audiences around the globe. They probably could not have survived as musicians without electronic reproduction. The advent of musical record-ing brought an explosion of interest in many genres, including jazz, country and western, and blues. Recording does increase the absolute rewards to Michael Jackson, as the superstars model suggests, but it also increases the absolute rewards to singers outside the mainstream. It is an open question whether the *relative* rewards of the superstars rise, as the superstars model predicts.

Superstars models assume an unambiguous definition of who is the most preferred or most meritorious performer. If we relax this assumption and introduce diversity of taste, electronic reproduction and economic growth can decentralize rewards. Electronic reproduction causes all fans to flock to the best performer only when fans agree on who is best. When fans prefer different idols, recording gives minority taste a stronger foothold in the marketplace. Performers respond by generating more creative and more diverse forms of music.

The most successful record albums (or CDs) and singles do not command an increasing share of the market over time, as measured by weeks on the chart. The dominant musical acts of the 1950s and 1960s enjoyed a high relative status that is harder to achieve today, given the greater competitiveness of the current market and the greater diversity of fan taste.

Consider the six biggest blockbuster albums since 1955, as defined by weeks spent at the number-one position on the *Billboard* charts. None was issued more recently than 1983. *West Side Story* spent 54 weeks at number one, starting in 1962; Michael Jackson's *Thriller*, released in 1983, spent 37 weeks at number one; the *South Pacific* soundtrack from 1958 spent 31 weeks at number one; and Harry Belafonte's *Calypso* album from 1956 spent 31 weeks at number one. Fleetwood Mac's *Rumours* and the *Saturday Night Fever* soundtrack are next in line, both from the late 1970s (the next two albums on the list are from 1984 and 1990). Today it is harder to achieve market domination. In the 1990s the number-one spot has been held by such diverse performers as Metallica (heavy metal), Michael Jackson (pop), Garth Brooks (country), Nirvana (grunge), Aerosmith (rock), Snoop Doggy Dogg (rap), and Ace of Base (Swedish pop).[3]

A deeper look at the album charts also shows an increase in diversity. I constructed a simple index (see note 4 for details) to measure the degree to which top albums dominated the market in each decade. For the 1955–1959 period this index figure was 37; it rose to 47.7 in the 1960s, a decade with many blockbuster albums. The figure fell to 18.6 in the 1970s, when few albums dominated the charts, rose again to 29.5 in the 1980s, but fell again to 21.3 in the 1990s. The 1950s and 1960s had far more blockbuster albums than more recent decades, as defined by relative domination of the market, and the 1990s have had fewer blockbuster albums than the 1980s. This evidence belies the claim that the superstar effect strengthens with increased reproducibility.[4]

The singles market shows similar trends, with one significant qualification. From 1955 to 1959, the top single in the average year held the top slot for 9 weeks. The figure fell to 6.4 weeks in the 1960s, to 6.2 weeks in the 1970s, and to 5.7 weeks in the 1980s, a consistent downward trend.

In the 1990–1996 period the figure rose sharply to 11 weeks, but this abrupt rise most likely reflects fundamental changes in the singles market, brought on by the nearly universal use of compact disks. In the 1990s the singles market became dominated by black and Latin artists, as mainstream white artists focused their efforts on the CD market. Through 1991, only two of the top singles in a year had been produced by black artists (Lionel Richie in 1985 and Roberta Flack in 1973, both relatively "white" black artists). In each year from 1992 to 1996, every top

The Proliferation of Fame

single was by a black or Latin artist and has enjoyed a high measure of market domination, relative to the situation in earlier years.[5]

Other facts from the *Billboard* charts illustrate the increasing decentralization of rewards in the music market. If we look at the number of songs that make the weekly charts in a year, the data for number-one hits and top-ten hits show that more songs crack these charts over time, implying that fewer top hits "hog" the charts for long periods. Overall, there is a general tendency toward more number-one hits each year and more top-ten hits each year. For instance, in 1948 there were only 9 number-one hits, but in 1989 there were 30; and while in 1948 there were only 57 top-ten hits, in 1989 there were 117. In relative terms, the top hits from recent times dominate the market less than earlier top hits did. Only for top-100 hits do we see evidence of a strengthening superstars effect: more songs reached the top 100 in the 1960s than in the 1980s, implying that a given song in the top 100 stays there longer today than previously.[6]

Television, a dominant part of today's culture, shows especially clear signs of fame decentralization. The growth of cable and satellite television has fragmented audiences. In the last fifteen years, the three major networks have lost 30 million viewers—a third of their audience. The TV show *Seinfeld*, considered the biggest hit of the 1990s, had an audience barely large enough to have placed it in the top twenty, had the number of viewers been compared to the number of viewers in a typical year in the 1970s.[7]

Movies provide another arena where we might expect to see a stronger superstars effect rather than growing diversity. Indeed, Robert Frank recently cited the cinema as an example of the obsession of modern culture with blockbusters. But again the available data, while limited, do not support the claim of an increasing centralization of returns. Let us track the box office gross of the top film in a year as a percentage of the gross of the top twenty-five films in the same year. If we start in 1980 (when the available data start), we find that the top film does not account for an increasing share of the market over time. Instead, the four years with the highest concentration of relative returns come at the first four years of the sample, 1980–1983. Even *Titanic*, the highest-grossing movie of all time, does not dominate the market as films did in the early 1980s; *The Empire Strikes Back*, released in 1980, was far more dominant. Nor does *Titanic*, released in 1997, herald an obvious trend toward an intensification of the superstars effect. The next year, 1998, was a strong year for the cinema, but no single blockbuster dominated the market.[8]

We can extend the sample back to 1957 by examining the ratio of the revenue of the biggest-grossing film of the year to the second biggest-grossing. But when we do that, we find no evidence of increasing centralization of rewards. The four times that the ratio is over 3.0 come in 1961, 1969, 1976, and 1977; even *Titanic* gets no more than a ratio of 2.37, relative to the take of the second most popular film that year, *Lost World*.[9]

The book publishing industry is based on reproducibility of the product, but again we see no evidence of a worsening superstars effect. The available data, running from 1973 on, show that the two years with the greatest sales concentration, as defined by the year's bestseller as a percentage of the top thirty books, are 1973 and 1975.[10]

After all, to view publishing in perspective, the advent of the printing press—a means of reproduction—has spurred diversity in literature and decentralized rewards. The reading and publishing of literature have been moving away from the superstars model for centuries. In the late sixteenth and early seventeenth centuries, John Foxe's *Book of Martyrs* dominated English reading. The *Book of Martyrs* circulated actively for at least 120 years and outsold all English language books except the Bible. John Bunyan's *Pilgrim's Progress,* published in 1678, attained a similar status. By 1792 Bunyan's work had been through 160 editions and had circulated in England and America almost as widely as the Bible. And the Bible itself was a literary superstar of earlier ages. Today no single author captures such a large share of the market. In 1990 alone, over two billion books were sold in the United States; the number of copies sold of the fifteen best-selling books throughout the entire 1980s accounts for less than 1 percent of this figure.[11]

Evidence from tennis, another field selected for superstar status by Frank and Cook, further belies the claim of increasing centralization. The distribution of prize money in tennis, across the top fifty performers, does not indicate a systematic trend over time, and in fact has become more decentralized over the last decade, as measured by the Gini coefficient, a traditional measure of inequality. The years when rewards became more concentrated are approximately the same years when television ratings declined, contrary to what the superstars model would predict.[12]

No comparisons of these kinds can provide definitive evidence for or against the superstars argument. I have, for instance, compared the number-one book to the top 30 books, but what about comparing the top 30 to the top 200 or 2,000 books? (The comparisons I made were limited by the amount of data available.) Given a broad enough sample, the people at the bottom are always earning zero. The superstars hypothesis, which postulates increasing inequality, becomes reduced to the simpler and less controversial claim that people at the top are earning more. In virtually every field, a large number of competitors at the bottom earn nothing. If absolute rewards rise for the top performers, there will exist a comparison for which the superstars argument appears to be true, even if we are witnessing an overall increase in cultural diversity and a decentralization of rewards among the successful performers. The higher positive returns, relative to the zero returns, will rise. More abstractly, there is no single correct and unambiguous measure of inequality; differing statistical measures may contradict each other, depending on a variety of factors, including how they adjust for and define the relevant population size. We therefore will never have a definitive statistical answer to questions raised by the superstars hypothesis. We can, however, ask whether modern consumers face a broader menu of choice with regard to our culture and with regard to heroes and celebrities. The answer to this question is "yes" in virtually every field.[13]

A Trickle-Down Economics of Fame?

Contrary to the predictions of the superstars model, the performances of the very best usually stimulate interest in the lesser players. Boris Becker's successes boosted interest in tennis in Germany, Tiger Woods has helped golfers across the board, and Bobby Fischer's rise to fame caused American chess to boom at all levels. Publicity for top stars creates trickle-down benefits for less popular performers, again decentralizing fame rewards.

When basketball fans watched Michael Jordan on television, they watched games against lesser teams, watched Jordan's lesser teammates, and developed interests in other players. Fans followed the National Basketball Association and its cast of characters just as they would have read installments of a novel. The minor and major characters, although they did not compete against each other in any single game, complemented each other's fame in the larger picture. Professional sports leagues package collective fame in appealing bundles.

If fans cared only about the superstars, the NBA would market one-on-one tournaments (Jordan vs. Barkley, Magic vs. Bird, Shaquille O'Neal vs. Tim Duncan) at the expense of team play. Instead the league creates institutions that allow teams and players to reflect and support each other's fame. Most fans would end up bored if the very best players squared off every night. Fans prefer to see a series of lesser contests, interrupted by occasional regular-season "previews" of the big match, leading up to a final championship confrontation. This sequence of events creates drama and mystery and supports the fame of lesser competitors in the process.[14]

The Convergence of Quality

Economic growth and the development of markets, including increasing reproduction, lead the quality of stars in a given area to converge over time, a development that tends to decentralize fame. In the heyday of Babe Ruth, the very best baseball players were *much* better than the worst or the middling players in the league. In 1920 Babe Ruth hit 54 home runs, more than any other *team* in the league; the next leading home run hitter hit only 19, and only one other *team* hit more than 44. Wilt Chamberlain, in the 1961–62 NBA season, *averaged* more than 50 points and 25 rebounds per game. Today these statistics would be extremely impressive and indeed astonishing as the achievements of one peak performance, much less as *averages*. Later Chamberlain scored 100 points in a single game and probably would have scored more had fans not ended the game by rushing onto the court. In another game he pulled down 55 rebounds. Today no player comes close to matching such statistics.[15]

Baseball hitting averages illustrate similar trends. Throughout this century, baseball hitting averages have not deviated much from .260; movements away from the average have been corrected by changes in the rules or changes in the size of the strike zone. Despite a roughly constant mean, however, the peaks have fallen consistently over time. No single baseball player has hit over .400 since Ted Williams performed the feat in 1941. Before that, a .400 batting average was relatively common; Ty Cobb, for instance, achieved it three times. In Cobb's day the quality of pitchers and hitters varied dramatically, and individual hitters were capable of astonishing statistical feats. Today's hitters are no worse and arguably are better, but they do not reach the same lone peaks. Even the new peaks we observe, such as in home run hitting for a single year, show a clustering of achievement (Mark McGwire, Sammy Sosa, and Ken Griffey) rather than a solo titan.[16]

When we watch Leni Riefenstahl's classic movie *Olympia*, shot during the 1936 Berlin Olympics, we are struck by the footage of the track and field events. What captures our attention is not the slowness of the runners but the vast gaps between the race winners and the second-place participants. Today's track and field events, by contrast, run the risk of producing excessively fine gradations between winners and losers. When Carl Lewis broke the world record for the 100-meter sprint in 1991, he won the race by only 0.002 of a second.

The first six runners were all within 0.11 of a second, the smallest gradation on a traditional stopwatch.[17]

The convergence of quality is easiest to observe in sports, where performance quality can be measured with relative ease, but similar mechanisms operate in most fields. Adam Smith was an intellectual giant who understood much more than most of his peers about economics. If we read the available texts, we can see a great difference between Smith and the twentieth best economist of his day. The analogous difference today is a very small one. Music, art, letters, and many other fields show a similar concentration of quality and competitive pressure.[18]

The convergence of performance quality limits the ability of the very best stars to dominate the market and reap all the fame. Baseball today has many excellent home run hitters, but no one of these hitters is identified with the home run the way that Babe Ruth was. Even if the total amount of "home run hitting fame" increases, the fame of the best-known slugger may not match the fame of Ruth. Babe Ruth's swing and bat size were mimicked by later sluggers, such as Jimmie Foxx and Rogers Hornsby, and soon the techniques became commonplace. In subsequent eras, no single player dominated home run hitting the way Ruth did, in part because other performers learned from Ruth's innovations. Pitchers studied Ruth as well, and they learned how to avoid serving up easy home run balls.

Reproducibility and economic growth increase salaries and fame, and this attracts more participants into a sport or genre, increases competitiveness, improves the quality of scouting and coaching, and draws in greater talent. The resulting rise in competitiveness brings all performers closer to a common performance mean. Relative to the earlier state of affairs, fame ends up more evenly distributed, rather than being concentrated in a few superstars. In the baseball of the 1920s and 1930s, minor league players often were better than major league players but the minor league player could not necessarily gain a promotion to the majors. The costs of information were high, scouting was poorly developed, and the number of minor league teams was large relative to the number of major league teams. Today a corresponding situation is unthinkable. Competitive markets bring the best performers to the fore while preventing any single performer from dominating the sport, as did Babe Ruth.[19]

The rise of many talented stars encourages fans to develop their tastes in non-mainstream directions. My favorite tennis player, Boris Becker, is no longer in the top ten, but I can still (circa 1999) watch him and see a very good tennis match. When many performers play very well, fans can follow a star who is not at the top without sacrificing much in terms of performance quality. The modern world gives fans greater scope to follow performers of their favorite nationality, style, or looks than did earlier times. In other words, reproducibility and economic growth, by increasing absolute performance levels, lower the cost of holding diverse or non-mainstream tastes. This factor decentralizes fame rewards, again contrary to the superstars argument.

In sum, the superstars model points to one possible tendency in fame markets, but countervailing tendencies operate as well. The evidence does not support the prediction of an unambiguously increasing concentration of rewards and therefore does not support pessimistic interpretations of the superstars model. Just as fame increases in quantity with economic growth, so it develops in multiple and diverse directions, reflecting many differing conceptions of merit.

IS FAME ZERO-SUM?

Other doctrines of "fame pessimism" suggest that fame and fame-seeking have declined or will decline. Some commentators claim that if fans or critics award more renown to one performer, some other performer must fall in relative standing by an equal amount. This view portrays fame as zero-sum in nature. Fame-seeking resembles a wasteful game of musical chairs, where one person's gain is another person's loss and the number of winners cannot be increased. Fred Hirsch wrote of "positional goods," which are necessarily fixed in supply, and he included status in his list. He viewed the pursuit of positional goods as a market failure. The superstars argument also views fame as zero-sum, by assuming that the fame of the superstar necessarily takes away from the renown of competing performers.[20]

On the surface the zero-sum fame assumption appears plausible. If one athlete wins the Most Valuable Player award in a given year, no other athlete can win the same award in that year. This example, however, is misleading. Fame does not differ from other economic goods in this regard. If I eat an apple or a slice of pizza, no other person can eat the same piece of food. Yet we do not conclude that food production is a zero-sum endeavor. Rather, the supply of food, like the supply of fame, grows over time with investment and technology. In economic terminology, fame supply is elastic. When fans demand more stars, and more performers seek stardom, markets bring the two parties together, increasing the amount and kinds of fame. The growing quest for fame meets a growing rather than a fixed supply.

Fans can give stars, in the aggregate, only a finite amount of attention, but we are not close to the point where this constraint bounds the total supply of fame. Many technologies, such as television and the Internet, enable fans to pay more attention to more stars by economizing fan time, energy, and information. The compact disk increases the number of musicians we follow. Furthermore, fans can spend more time following the famous by devoting less effort to non–fame-producing endeavors. The more attractive it becomes to follow famous performers of various kinds, the less time fans will spend mowing the lawn.

It is sometimes alleged that fame would not be worth very much if everyone were famous. Even if this claim were true (I, for one, still would enjoy the adulation), fame remains positive-sum *at its current margin*. Although fame is growing in supply, it is not close to being so plentiful as to lose its exclusive flavor and its power. Modern manifestations of fame and celebrity exercise no less attraction and caché than before, even though the ranks of the famous have grown.

HOW FANS STIMULATE FAME PRODUCTION

Fans' desires for information, evaluation, and enthusiasm create incentives for critics to coin new awards, augment the meaning of old ones, and promote new stars. The critics who produce new kinds of fame for fans draw attention and dollars at the expense of critics who do not. This competitive rivalry pushes the market for fame in new directions and augments the supply of fame.

The rise of country and western music brought C&W Halls of Fame, C&W fan clubs, C&W music magazines with annual awards, and many other forms of organized approbation for the genre. These institutions were created to capture the attention of C&W fans, thereby generating status and profit. Similarly, entrepreneurs frequently start new Halls of Fame; the first Hall of Fame was created in 1901, and America now has over 600 Halls. Most of these Halls induct individuals on a periodic basis and thus are growing in size, again to attract and maintain fan interest. Several decades ago, British writers could win only a few literary prizes, but now they can compete for almost fifty, most of which are awarded annually and many of which are accompanied by significant public recognition. These prizes have stimulated interest in many of the nominees, not just the award winners. The NBA now defines a first team, second team, and third team of best players each year, as well as an all-defensive team, instead of just bestowing a Most Valuable Player award, as in the past. The Grammy Awards create new categories as music develops.[21]

The *World Dictionary of Awards and Prizes* outlines thousands of awards and prizes, all of which, obviously, were new at some point. The Wyld Propulsion Award goes to a scientist for notable work in the service of rocket propulsion, the Yant Award is for non-U.S. contributors to the science of industrial hygiene, and the Logie Award goes yearly to the outstanding male and female personalities in Australian television. Every four years the International Institute for Refrigeration awards a prize for scientific research in their area.

Not only are new prizes created, but critics redefine the meaning and stature of old prizes. The World Cup has become an epic, fame-producing contest since its origin in 1930. The first few competitions attracted relatively little public attention and produced little fame at the time. In fact it was difficult to get most countries to send squads; only four European countries sent teams to Uruguay for the first Cup in 1930. Over time the succession of stars, dramatic match-ups, and heroic performances have created a special caché for a World Cup victory. The 1998 French winners now share in the glory of Pele, Franz Beckenbauer, and Diego Maradona. This ongoing redefinition of the meaning of the World Cup has not been automatic; it has required critical interpretation and marketing. Critics seek to make effective and illuminating comparisons to increase their own stature and therefore they draw the attention of fans to the depth and meaning of previous contests.[22]

THE ROLE OF STATISTICS

Fans and critics boost the supply of fame by improving their abilities to measure performance. Athletes can achieve fame by besting competitors from the past and their own prior performances. Roger Bannister was the first person to run a mile in under four minutes. Hank Aaron hit 758 home runs in his career, breaking Babe Ruth's previous record of 714. Wayne Gretzky holds hockey records for goals, assists, and points, both for an individual season and for an entire career.

The Guinness Book of World Records, a strong seller for many years, produces fame through a compendium of statistical achievements. The book has entries for the longest fingernails (224 inches on five fingers), the most expensive print (a Rembrandt, sold for $786,000), and the largest painting (92,419 square feet, completed in Amsterdam in 1996). People go to great lengths to document their achievements and make sure they are recognized by the Guinness, knowing that statistics provide a clear and focal measure of achievement.

Organizations take deliberate steps to increase the importance of measurement and records in sports. When the modern Olympics were initiated in 1896, some observers complained that gymnastics were unpopular because performance could not be measured. The Olympics subsequently implemented a scale for grading the performance of gymnasts based on the rankings of judges. The Rumanian gymnast Nadia Comaneci became famous for achieving perfect "10s." In similar fashion, baseball created a new statistic, the save, to measure the achievements of relief pitchers. The National Basketball Association created the statistic of the blocked shot to measure defensive prowess. Sabermetricians—people who apply econometrics to sports—have created new and complex statistics to weight a player's overall performance by aggregating other numerical measures through complex formulas. Bill James, an insightful baseball analyst, has helped resurrect the fame of Lefty Grove, a pitcher who otherwise might have remained underrated.[23]

Note that statistics, in addition to creating new categories of fame, lower the costs of organizing fandoms. Like a fan club or critic, a statistic coordinates fan response to the quality of performance. If fans treat statistics as measures of quality, and if each fan varies his or her approval with statistical performance, fans will act in a coordinated fashion and strengthen their influence. The statistic serves as a silent critic by creating a single, influential standard.[24]

THE SHUTTLECOCK OF FAME

As the world becomes wealthier and more diverse, standards for fame become more complex and more heterogeneous. The resulting uncertainty about the quality of performers results in more fame. Critics and fans debate whether Muhammad Ali, Joe Frazier, or George Foreman would have had the best chance against Joe Louis, but they will never know. Continued uncertainty about their relative merits helps sustain the fame of all four boxers and gives fans and critics something to argue about. Those who are against war may promote the renown of Ali, an opponent of the Vietnam War, whereas the culturally conservative may argue for the chances of Joe Louis. These motives to promote the fighters' reputations would be weaker if fans and critics knew who would win the hypothetical fight. Sports performers achieve more fame when athletic quality cannot be precisely measured. Samuel Johnson noted that fame is a shuttlecock that needs determined opposition from enemies to keep it in contention.[25]

Many kinds of achievement are multidimensional. Although Roger Maris and Hank Aaron each broke one of Babe Ruth's home run records, fans still question whether Maris and Aaron were superior home run hitters. No contest, even a hypothetical one, can resolve the question. Maris had only two spectacular slugging years and Aaron broke Ruth's career record by playing more years, rather than by having a greater frequency of home runs per times at bat. But Aaron and Maris did face better pitchers than Ruth did. Other fans may defend the slugging skills of Ted Williams and Harmon Killebrew, pointing to their high ratios of home runs per times at bat. How Sosa and McGwire will fare in the debate remains to be seen. Tennis fans often argue about whether the formidable backhand of Andre Agassi would have proved a match for the forehand of John McEnroe when both players were at the top of the game.[26]

Fiberglass poles allow the today's pole-vaulters to jump higher than the athletes of 1950, but they also give previous stars, who used wooden poles, a permanent place in history. Similarly, baseball's move from a 154-game season to a 162-game season made Babe Ruth's sixty home runs in 1927 a more secure record (at least until McGwire and Sosa bested the record in fewer than 154 games). When Roger Maris hit sixty-one home runs in 1961, his achievement entered the record books with an asterisk, noting that Maris had had the chance to play more games than Ruth did.

Critics manufacture suspense to increase the value of awards, building up to the revelation of a winner. The awarders of the Booker Prize publish a "short list" before announcing the winner, to fuel speculation and debate. The interest of the British betting industry in these proceedings and the willingness of bookies to offer and publish odds illustrate the success of this tactic. The Academy Awards also rely on nominations—which are analogous to the short list—to stimulate interest, discussion, and rumor. Less fame would be produced if we knew for sure who was the best actor in a given year.[27]

THE COMPLEMENTARY NATURE OF FAME

Rivalries often produce fame for both parties to the contest, rather than merely redistributing fame, as the zero-sum view would suggest. The duel of Mark McGwire and Sammy Sosa sparked great interest, as the two battled for single-season home run supremacy. Carl Lewis and Ben Johnson became the two most prominent track runners of the late twentieth century through their repeated confrontations. Magic Johnson and Larry Bird increased their renown through their basketball rivalry in the 1980s. Muhammad Ali owes part of his fame to having had the opportunity to fight Sonny Liston, Joe Frazier, and George Foreman, all worthy opponents. The more recent Mike Tyson has not had opponents of similar stature, and consequently his long-run reputation as a fighter probably will suffer, even though he dominated boxing for a number of years. We all know The Three Tenors—Placido Domingo,

Luciano Pavarotti, and José Carreras. Each of these men has become more famous through the renown of the others.

Rankings produce information and help establish the reputation of a performer in the first place. Critics and fans produce fame by comparing one performer to others and by setting standards within the context of previous achievements. When evaluating Beethoven, critics compare the quantity and quality of his output to the quantity and quality of the music composed by Mozart, Haydn, and others. If critics had heard only the music of Beethoven, and not that of other composers, they would not know how much fame to award him. *Comparisons* indicate that Beethoven's Ninth Symphony is an extraordinary masterpiece rather than an average work. As for Haydn, even if he ends up ranked lower than Beethoven, knowledge of Beethoven still helps us see virtues in Haydn's compositions. Comparisons indicate that Haydn is relatively close to the best, even if he himself is not the best.

Comparisons augment the total supply of fame by producing information for fans and critics. If comparisons were impossible, judgments would be less definite and the total amount of renown would be lower. Fans and critics make a comparison with the express purpose of producing more knowledge and increasing the supply of fame. In addition, comparative information directs fan attention toward fame-generating activities and away from non–fame-generating activities. The classical music evaluations of the *Penguin Guide* help fans spend their money effectively when they buy CDs and thereby spur fame for composers and conductors. In the absence of such rankings, fans might instead spend their time and money in activities that produce less or no fame, such as knitting or gardening.

Plutarch portrayed fame as complementary rather than strictly rivalrous and stressed that comparisons illuminate individual virtues. His *Lives* offers direct comparisons of famous Greeks and famous Romans; some chapters have titles such as "Comparison of Poplicola with Solon." Plutarch wanted to show that Roman history was no less illustrious than Greek history. To this end he created a new canon of heroes to compare with the Greeks. In the very first paragraph of his *Lives* Plutarch cited Aeschylus:

Whom shall I set so great a man to face?
Or whom oppose? Who's equal to the place?

Plutarch saw the Romans as the equal of the Greeks *and* believed that elevating the reputation of the Romans would not detract from the renown of the Greeks. Rather, the Greeks and the Romans reflect and mirror each other's virtues. Imitation, Plutarch thought, was indeed the sincerest form of flattery, a way of paying homage that demonstrates the favorable qualities of both the model and the imitator. Of Solon, for instance, Plutarch wrote, "Solon may thus be said to have contributed to Poplicola's glory, so did also Poplicola to his, by his choice of him as his model." Later, Plutarch wrote of great men that they were like a looking glass, in which we may see how to "adjust and adorn" our own lives.[28]

In a similar fashion Virgil presented the competition for fame as a positive-sum game. In *The Aeneid,* Virgil uses the glory of the Greeks to illustrate the grandeur of the Romans. In his version of Rome's founding, the losing Greeks from Troy play a critical role, and Greek themes reverberate throughout the poem.

Fame can also be expanded by the accumulation of prize-winners. Some prizes increase in value as more people receive them. If only one writer ever received the Nobel Prize, the prize would not be worth very much, either to the prize committee or to the winner. When only one award is made for all time, audiences do not pay much attention.

The Barnard Medal, awarded by the National Academy of Arts and Sciences and Columbia University for distinctive achievements in physics, is given only once every five years. Although many distinguished scientists have received the medal (Enrico Fermi, Ernest Rutherford, Albert Einstein, and Niels Bohr, to name a few), it is not very well known. The medal simply is not awarded frequently enough to generate regular publicity. Some electors to the baseball Hall of Fame have feared that the public might lose interest in the Hall if too few new entrants were chosen. One journalist wrote, "Baseball has plenty of great stars and figures of whom it is proud. To have the Hall of Fame only half filled gives the impression that the game is short of talent."[29]

The stature and the prestige of Nobel Prizes has increased over time. In the early years, the prizes received little attention from either the general public or the scientific community. Both the popular press and the scientific journals gave only scant notice to prize announcements. Foreign scientists, when invited to nominate candidates, usually failed to reply. The prizewinners themselves, in response to a questionnaire circulated ten years after the inception of the prizes, cited the benefits of the money rather than the honor of the recognition. The stature of the prizes grew only slowly, and only after the committees had established a track record of honoring distinguished men and women who would reflect credit on the prizes themselves. Similarly, the Pulitzer Prizes received little attention until they had established a reputation for excellence.[30]

Great ages, eras, and movements further illustrate the complementary nature of fame. Many creators or leaders who would have been insignificant figures had they labored in isolation achieved renown by participating in collective trends or movements—think of the Age of Pericles, the Age of Augustus, the Florentine Renaissance, early-twentieth-century Modernism, and Abstract Expressionism. The Bible combines a variety of stories to produce fame for characters who would otherwise have achieved less renown; biblical "stars" such as Abraham, Job, and Cain make each other more famous.[31]

The complementarity of fame stems partially from the fixed costs behind the production of reputation. It is much cheaper to produce one large *Who's Who in America* than to print and distribute a separate and (much) smaller volume for each person. Producing fame in collective packages lowers costs and leads to wider dissemination. Readers, listeners, and other fame consumers concentrate their attention on particular books, genres, historical epochs, sports, and so forth, rather than sampling the life stories of individual stars one by one. Efficient and insightful fame packaging therefore draws great fan attention. Fame complementarities are not simply "out there"; they are created through critical persuasion and instruction, and through dialogue with fans.

Intermediaries—such as the NBA, educators, historians, storytellers, preachers, and myth-makers—have reasons for constructing appealing packages of fame complementarity. Network announcers try to sell fans on the notion that during his career Magic Johnson faced a series of epic match-ups with Julius Erving, Larry Bird, Isiah Thomas, and Michael Jordan. Critics and commentators paint a picture of immediate rivalry and long-term fame complementarity, thus creating an ongoing lineage of competitive rivalries and maintaining or augmenting the value of their interpretative franchise. A once-and-for-all fame tournament, by contrast, would put the critic or intermediary out of business quickly. Critics therefore support the construction of a social "web of fame" with durable, complementary parts.

Fans, critics, and organizing bodies use the pooling and separation of competitors to produce more fame. In sports, fans and critics use leagues, divisions, conferences, runoffs, and playoffs to achieve the most intriguing match-ups and comparisons. The National Collegiate Athletic Association defines a variety of conference champions in addition to the winner of the yearly tournament. Boxing defines twelve separate weight divisions, ranging from flyweight to heavyweight, each with separate titles and competitions. These weight divisions are more finely grained than would be needed to ensure competitive balance in a given fight. Flyweights, for instance, cannot exceed 112 pounds, Bantamweights cannot exceed 118 pounds, Junior Featherweights cannot exceed 122 pounds, Featherweights cannot exceed 126 pounds, and Junior Lightweights cannot exceed 130 pounds. Individuals who differ by as little as 13 pounds, for instance, may be separated by three weight classes. The proliferation of titles allows more fame to be produced.[32]

Organizing bodies segregate by sex and age to assist the production of glory. Chris Evert would have been less famous, and her fans would have been less happy, had she been regularly trounced by John McEnroe in tennis tournaments. Evert's loss of fame, from losing to him, would have exceeded McEnroe's gain in fame, from beating her. Seniors' tournaments are prominent on the golf circuit, where Arnold Palmer can maintain a public profile without losing to numerous "lesser" younger players. Fame-producing intermediaries limit potential incidences of negative-sum fame by creating separate tournaments and segregated categories of evaluation. The unlikelihood of negative-sum fame is no accident; it follows directly from the active intervention of critics and organizers.

Fame packaging can create the possible thrill of an underdog victory. In 1954 the small high school of Milan (161 students) defeated the larger high school of Muncie Central High (2,200 students) in a game that remains legendary in Indiana and was celebrated in the 1986 movie *Hoosiers.* In 1996, however, the Indiana High School Athletic Association voted to abolish the statewide basketball tournament and to replace it with four separate tournaments, each for schools of comparable size. Under the new arrangement, small schools are spared losing to larger schools, and have some chance of winning a championship in a small-school division. But this decision aroused furor in Indiana. Opponents of the decision organized a petition of high school principals to have the decision overturned (but lost), claiming that small schools can never prove themselves under the new system. Older residents and spectators, many of whom still remember the Milan triumph, favor the greater glory produced by the statewide tournament. One seventy-three-year-old retired administrator remarked, "I still like one thing: either you're the big dog or you're not." Indeed the *Hoosiers* movie itself, made thirty-two years after the original upset, illustrates how memorable upsets can produce lasting fame.[33]

The best means of pooling and packaging will change with the relative abilities of performers. In the early days of computer chess, computers were not very skillful, and little fame could be produced by matching the best human player against the best computer. In 1996, however, the computer Deep Blue played a match against the world champion, Garry Kasparov, and won the first game. Kasparov, however, came back to win the match. Kasparov had already routed several human contenders for the World Chess Championship, including Anatoly Karpov, and could do little more to augment his fame, at least until he beat Deep Blue. The second match, held in 1997, was won by Deep Blue, although only because Kasparov made uncharacteristic errors. The theme of man versus machine produced a new level of interest for chess fans and stimulated interest in the game at all levels. Once computers manage to beat world chess champions regularly, however, competitive segmentation will reemerge as the dominant means of fame production in chess.

The production of fame through bundling, like so many other fame-producing mechanisms, may push renown further away from merit. Many American sports fans, if asked what has been the greatest baseball team of all time, or at least the greatest team of earlier eras, would pick the 1927 New York Yankees. This team had Babe Ruth and Lou Gehrig, as well as Tony Lazzeri, Earle Combs, Bob Meusel, Waite Hoyt, Herb Pennock, and Urban Shocker. From 1926 through 1928 the Yankees compiled a record of 302–160. The Philadelphia Athletics of 1929–1931, however, were arguably the superior team. They had a three-year record of 313–143, better than the Yankees', and won the World Series twice in three years. The team had Jimmie Foxx, Al Simmons, Mickey Cochrane, George Earnshaw, Rube Walberg, and Lefty Grove. At the time most people thought the Athletics were the better team. Why then have the Yankees achieved greater fame? One reason is that the Yankees continued a winning tradition over several decades and built a dynasty. The Athletics, by contrast, sold off their best players shortly after the 1931 season. The Yankees remained in New York and built a history. The Athletics moved to Kansas City, and then to Oakland. In short, the Yankees bundled their history better than did other baseball teams and thus acquired more fame, whether they deserve it or not.[34]

THE BURDEN OF THE PAST

Some commentators have put forth an argument that is, in effect, an intertemporal version of the superstars hypothesis. This idea, popular in the eighteenth century, claims that fame-seekers are intimidated by the impressive array of past performances. Current performers feel "the Burden of the Past"—a phrase coined by Walter Jackson Bate—and refrain from pursuing fame. The relevant superstars already have been produced, and no fame remains to be earned. At most there is temporary celebrity.

Johann Wolfgang Goethe wrote, "Had I known [in writing *Werther* and *Faust*] as clearly as I now do how much that is excellent has been in existence for hundreds and thousands of years, I would not have written a line, but would have done something else." According to one story, possibly apocryphal, a Japanese archery sport was abandoned in the seventeenth century after one archer put on a spectacular performance that could never be equaled. David Hume wrote of the end of fame-seeking in a world where "the posts of honour are all occupied." Hume believed that the excellence of Italian paintings inhibited the development of English art, that Greek attainments stifled the initiative of the Romans, and that the achievements of the French constrained the Germans.[35]

The nineteenth-century literary critic and essayist William Hazlitt also argued that the motivation to seek fame would weaken over time. In his 1814 essay "Why the Arts are not

Progressive—A Fragment," Hazlit claimed that the founders of a genre tend to be the most creative and accomplished. In earlier times men of genius faced little competition and were virtually assured of achieving great fame. Later creators have become "lost in the crowd of competitors," and they have a smaller chance of gaining recognition for their efforts.[36] .

But despite these arguments, the burden of the past does not make current stars give up the quest for fame. If we view fame as a tournament, the burden of the past implies that the tournament is harder to win. But if a person is intent on becoming famous, he or she may simply try harder. Some people will invest more resources and expend more effort in seeking fame the more difficult it becomes to achieve.

In other words, strong rivalries often spur rather than discourage fame-seeking. In sports tournaments the best players usually try their hardest when the field is strong rather than weak; intense competition spurs the best onward to more glorious and noble endeavors. The concentration of artistic achievements in particular points of space and time (Periclean Athens, the Florentine Renaissance, the Parisian art world) reflects the fact that competition promotes rather than discourages star efforts.[37]

The first author to talk about the burden of the past, the Roman Ammianus Marcellinus, suggested an answer to the dilemma. The past, he said, induces innovation, rather than choking it off. If creators cannot challenge the achievements of the past, they seek "new themes" instead. Eighteenth-century Scottish commentators on David Hume, such as Lord Kames, John Millar, Archibald Alison, and Alexander Gerard, made a similar point. They cited innovation as a means of continually replenishing the supply of fame.[38]

Past achievements often provide a springboard for current fame-seekers, rather than drying fame up. Performers who desire fame therefore may, counter-intuitively, seek out areas already rich in achievement. Fame-seekers try to innovate, but usually within established canons and genres, rather than starting from scratch. Sectors and endeavors that are "thick" with achievement can produce fame more easily through complementarities and collective fame packaging. Many Americans have heard of Sir Edmund Hillary, the first man to scale Mount Everest, but they would be hard pressed to name many other mountaineers. By contrast, most people less than fifty years old can name several dozen rock-and-roll stars, perhaps even several hundred. Rock and roll is thicker with public achievement than is mountaineering, at least in the United States. Rock and roll supports a well-known culture, many landmarks of past history and reference points, and a well-visited Hall of Fame. Given the complementary nature of fame, it may be harder to receive recognition for performing a unique feat with no close counterparts.

6   The Dark Side of Fame

By creating and spreading fame, markets make performers and performances extremely visible to fans and critics. Contrary to the zero-sum idea discussed in the previous chapter, markets sometimes produce too much fame. The spread and intensification of fame make society less private, more harried, and in certain regards less creative and diverse—the Faustian bargains of modern renown.

Markets are very poor at producing anonymity and invisibility for celebrities; very well known stars cannot buy the gift of "being left alone in public" at any price. Celebrities cannot walk into a movie theater or restaurant without causing a commotion and being deluged by attention. Bystanders flock around them, touch them, prod them, speak to them, and request favors, autographs, and friendships. Some fans aggressively track down stars and follow their movements closely. They buy printed materials that locate stars' homes, indicate when stars are in town or away, and list the phone numbers of stars.

It is no wonder that Woody Allen's *Stardust Memories* presents fans as a plague, or that Tyrone Power referred to his fans as "the monster." The former football player Tim Green wrote, "When it comes to fans, most players would rather shake hands with a leper."[1]

Journalists and photographers—effectively serving as the agents of fans—follow stars, stake out their residences, and call them at home at all hours of the night. During her tenure in Kensington Palace, Princess Diana was stalked by approximately fifty freelance photographers. Other photographers disguised themselves as window washers, strawberry pickers, and fellow vacationers. When Diana worked out in her health club, the club manager allowed a hidden camera to be placed to photograph her. Top-notch photos brought in as much as several million dollars each.[2]

The first wax museums and exhibits gave most citizens their first chance to see how the famous looked. That was the selling point of the exhibits. When Madame Tussaud brought her show from France to England in 1802, citizens flocked to gaze at the countenances of the wax figurines. Today's wax museums display faces that everyone can recognize. Rather than finding their looks revealing, we compare the wax dummies to the well-known media images of the same stars, commenting on how good or bad a job the sculptors have done.[3]

Privacy, by its nature, cannot be purchased easily in markets. In most cases individuals must make themselves at least partially visible to trade, but visibility counters the very purpose of buying privacy. A star who contacted reporters to buy their silence, for instance, would attract great attention through this very maneuver, even if he or she used intermediaries. Nor would a perfectly encrypted message do the trick, since it would have to specify *whose* privacy is being sought. In addition, any star who tries to pay fans or reporters to stay away will find many fans and reporters on her trail, looking to be paid off. Anonymity is best achieved by *doing nothing*, a strategy inconsistent with the nature of stardom.

Rather than bidding for their privacy, stars invest in high fences, nontransparent limousine windows, and bodyguards. These protections, in addition to being imperfect, are themselves newsworthy and stimulate further interest in the star. The quest for privacy therefore is partially self-frustrating. The more a star seeks privacy, the greater the demand for information about his or her reclusive and mysterious persona. J. D. Salinger, Thomas Pynchon, and Stanley Kubrick pursued such "isolationist" strategies, as did Salman Rushdie (albeit for other reasons). Information about these stars has become an exclusive and highly sought after commodity.

The desire of many stars to retreat is understandable, because lack of privacy makes stars vulnerable to pathological and violent fans. The line between extreme respect and extreme detestation is often a fine one; both "fan" and "fanatic" are derived from the same root. Many stars, including Clark Gable, Marilyn Monroe, and John Lennon have been hounded by an entourage of fans; their residences were under constant surveillance for many years. For five years a crazy fan pitched a tent outside Joni Mitchell's house. David Letterman was stalked by a crazy woman who suffered from erotomania. Michael J. Fox received over five thousand threatening letters from a single fan. Andy Warhol was shot by a crazed fan (although he survived), and Selena, the Hispanic singer, was fatally shot by the former president of her fan club. John Lennon, Piero Pasolini, and most of the Presidents who were assassinated lost their lives because of their fame. Monica Seles was stabbed by a crazed fan of Steffi Graf's for the ostensible reason of helping Steffi regain her number-one position.[4]

Even from the point of view of fans (much less that of stars), stars may become too visible to the public. When the star loses too much privacy, he or she may become less productive, less creative, and more hostile to fan interest, making all fans worse off. Star privacy is a "common pool" (as discussed in Chapter 4), which fans exhaust too rapidly and too thoroughly. No single fan can reap or internalize the benefits from leaving behind some "star privacy" for others to benefit from. Each fan prefers to observe stars, but a collectively undesirable outcome results when too many fans observe with too much intensity.

Similarly, collective action may misfire when it comes to the observation of automobile accidents. Each passing driver wishes to look at the accident, usually out of morbid curiosity. Yet when all drivers look, traffic slows down and all drivers end up worse off. The drivers, who do not have regular contact with each other, cannot make a collectively binding agreement that no one should look. Everyone looks, and everyone curses the delays that result.

FAME AND CREATIVITY

Diminishing privacy limits the creativity of performers and the diversity of society. Performers who are prominent tend to produce different kinds of work than do performers who remain hidden from public view. Obscure performers have unique visions and pursue their own creative ideas without being sidetracked by public opinion or by critics. As David Hume wrote, "Reputation is often as great a fascination upon men as sovereignty, and is equally destructive to the freedom of thought and examination."[5]

Markets cannot easily direct purchasing power toward buying outputs produced by "hidden performers." Even when the demand for such outputs is high, trading for them destroys their obscurity and thus makes their production visible. Just as stars cannot easily buy privacy, fans cannot easily buy the outputs of "invisible" performers. Markets are poorly suited to keeping secrets.

Naive Art is one genre where publicity and fame-seeking have not had much influence on behavior. Until recently, even the best Naive artists were not famous. By definition, Naive Art is created by untrained "amateurs," and is uninformed by traditional approaches to perspective. A typical Naive work uses bright colors, blunt shapes, and a distorted sense of depth and relative size to portray rural farm scenes or family members. The genre has until recently been neglected by professional critics, who tend to judge artworks in terms of classical standards of taste.[6] In the last few decades, however, Naive Art has attained high status as an innovative pictorial tradition. Entrepreneurial critics and dealers have realized that the best Naive works are among the most creative and provocative works of their time. Naive Art has become popular.

Although Naive works continue to rise in price and critical acclaim, this development is not entirely favorable for the genre. The recognition of Naive artworks threatens the virtues that produced its initial charm and vibrancy. The earlier absence of fame, by default, shaped Naive styles. Naive artists created to please themselves or local acquaintances, rather than to achieve widespread acclaim. Their creativity developed apart from outside critical influences and apart from desires to cater to large audiences. Naive works reflect the inner inspiration of the artist's mind to an especially high degree, rather than the pursuit of external canons of taste. Naive Art was essentially art without fame.

Elijah Pierce, one of America's most respected Naive artists, worked most of his life as a barber and a preacher. He had no formal training and first started making carvings to amuse his wife; he once said, "I didn't even know I was an artist 'til they told me." During the formative years of Pierce's art, he labored in total obscurity, developing his signature style. Today Pierce's barbershop is an art gallery, he receives visitors from around the world, he has been the subject of numerous magazine articles and short films, he has won international prizes, and he is revered in his own community for his achievement.[7]

Many other Naive artists had no expectations of fame. Ralph Griffin, an African American in the rural South, worked for several decades as a janitor in a local bakery. Only after he was fifty years old did he start carving driftwood. Edward Mumma, a retired farmer and antiques dealer, started painting when he was sixty-one, while recovering from an operation to remove cataracts. Henry Darger, now one of the best-known Outsider figures, worked as a janitor in Chicago and showed a total lack of concern with fame. Only after Darger died in 1973 did his landlord, while cleaning out his apartment, discover that Darger had created a 19,000-page illustrated saga entitled *The Story of the Vivian Girls in What Is Known as the Realms of the Unreal or the Glandelinian War Storm or the Glandico-Abbienian Wars as Caused by the Child Slave Rebellion,* now considered a pictorial classic.[8]

Since these artists now *have* achieved recognition, Naive Art cannot easily re-create the conditions of its initial success. Subsequent artists, while they may be Naive in the sense of lacking formal training, often set out with the desire to earn fame as Naive artists. They pitch their works to the critics who evaluate the merits of Naive Art, rather than pursuing the inner logic of their creativity. Artists now try to produce art in deliberately "Naive" styles, thus robbing Naive Art of its initial vitality. American Naive Art is now more visible than ever before.

For some creators, maintaining invisibility supports diversity and innovation. The amateur writer or social scientist faces different constraints, views the world in different ways, and develops different kinds of ideas than does the professional. The amateur may be a fame-*seeker*, but probably has little current reputation and faces little peer scrutiny. The amateur therefore is inclined to take more chances and to feel less constrained by orthodox opinion, and is more willing to think big. Although amateurs tend to be sloppier and less rigorous than professionals, innovation is encouraged when some amateurs, rather than exclusively professionals, are engaged in creative endeavors. If all performers are watched closely by critics and fans, some new ideas will have a harder time winning a hearing.[9]

Greater visibility can lower quality by producing excessively large audiences. Thomas Nagel points to the contrast between the public roles played by French intellectuals and those played by philosophers in the English-speaking world. Leading French philosophers are public figures, and they compete for wide literary fame by offering opinions on many subjects. Their income and status, to some extent, depend upon the reactions of the broader public. American philosophers rarely have a high public profile, and they usually write for fellow academicians. The American system risks "arid technicalities," whereas the French system risks "oversimplification and fake profundity." The American system does not dispense with fame, since philosophers still win renown from their peers. Nonetheless, by restricting fame to a small circle of admirers, the American system produces an intellectual rigor that the French system does not.[10]

Fame may have decreased the quality of professional basketball. Players emphasize slam-dunking and other acrobatic moves at the expense of sound fundamentals and quality team play. Slam-dunking puts the player in the week's highlight film, but sound dribbling, passing, and defense do not. In essence, fame-seeking players overemphasize the visible at the expense of substance. Star players, rather than good teams, receive increasing publicity, thus encouraging flashy play, even at the expense of the team. Many of the league's young stars are extraordinarily gifted athletes and make spectacular plays, but do not exhibit sound fundamentals. To some extent, consumers and fans simply get what they want; viewers may prefer a flashy, fun game to a well-played game. Nonetheless the quality of team play and fundamentals may be public goods for the league as a whole. The league benefits from well-played games, but no single player tries very hard to produce this collective benefit, since it yields little private fame.[11]

Diversity, creativity, and quality develop most freely if fame and fame-seeking do not reign in every genre. The genres without fame-seeking—such as Naive Art, at least until recently—will produce styles and kinds of achievements that other more fame-oriented genres cannot. An analogous point holds for the commercialization of the arts. Even if commercialization is desirable, all things considered, the ideal state of affairs involves some noncommercialized genres, if only to produce aesthetic diversity. Such an ideal may not be attainable, given the tendency of commercialization to spread, but the ideal does give us a standard against which to measure the imperfections of modern culture.

Many creators structure their environment to avoid the influence of external approbation, so that their creativity will flourish and thier technical rigor will not be diluted. Paul Gauguin moved to the South Sea islands to paint. When Marcel Proust was writing *Remembrance of Things Past*, he remained in his room with cork-lined walls and refused to receive visitors for more than fifteen minutes a day. The Beatles gave up touring and extensive public appearances to make their greatest albums, such as *Sgt. Pepper*. They wanted both the extra time and freedom from having to please the crowd every day. Glenn Gould gave up concertizing to concentrate on making recordings. Yet the long reach of contemporary fame makes such escapes increasingly difficult and costly. In today's world, the stratagems of Gauguin and Proust would guarantee publicity rather than isolation.

In addition, performers cannot easily cease caring and thinking about the opinions of critics and fans, no matter how hard they try to do so. Hiding from the public eye is not the same thing as ignoring popular and critical opinion. The stars who shut out the public are arguably those who care *most* about their reputations; they reject the public first in a preemptive strike because they live in fear the public will reject them. The momentum of fame incentives and reputational concerns is difficult to check. Just as stars cannot easily buy privacy, they cannot easily make themselves indifferent to public and critical opinion.

The extension and intensification of fame, in addition to limiting creativity, strips away mystery and discovery. If fans know everything about the lives of stars, including their sex lives and their innermost secrets, the fans' own lives may become poorer as a result. A fame-intensive society loses the ability to create awe through the revelation of surprises.

The concept of surprise is increasingly diluted as more and more secrets are revealed and shock follows shock. Individual critics reveal successive bits of information about sex, violence, and other topics of interest to fans. Each critic gains by attracting audience attention, but the net result is an inflation of our standards for surprise, interest, and mystery. Performers find it increasingly difficult to achieve a particular emotional effect when the audience already knows a great deal about their public and private lives. And excesses blunt the effect of even greater excesses: If one movie shows a star violently killing three hundred enemies, how much greater is the impact of four hundred dead enemies in the next movie? How much more can be shown than full frontal nudity? What more can fans know about a star once they know about his or her sex life?

The diminution of surprise plagues the aesthetic realm as well. We can no longer look at Leonardo's *Mona Lisa* or hear Mozart's Symphony no. 40 with full freshness. These creations have become so famous that they are overexposed. The common pool of their aesthetic surprise and vitality has been overfished. One Manhattan gallery is now selling rugs with Naive Art patterns on them; as these rugs achieve wider circulation, Naive images will lose some of their surprising nature as well.

Overfamiliarity, combined with cynical and repetitious debunkings, may displace the fascination with the truly new. In the long run, a culture saturated with overfamiliarity becomes less hopeful, less interested, and less erotic, as the sense of discovery weakens. Many of the famous are like magicians. They lose their ability to excite us if their creations become too familiar and subject to regular scrutiny.[12]

FAME AND RISK

To the extent that fame prizes are valuable, people will take great prospective risks to win them. A fame-intensive society therefore encourages innovation at the early stages of careers. Up-and-coming performers will try any and all means to rise to the top, given how much winning is worth. They will take chances with styles, media of presentation, aesthetics, and so on.[13]

At the same time, established stars will take fewer risks. Once performers become famous, many seek to hold onto their dominant market positions and become less likely to produce radical innovations. The higher the value of fame, the more famous people have to lose by slipping and the greater the impetus for conservatism. Many of the benefits of fame can be enjoyed even after the performer's creativity has dried up. The surviving members of Led Zeppelin, for instance, have remained in great demand even after the creativity of the group's work declined and the group split up. The former group members Jimmy Page and Robert Plant need only avoid disgracing themselves to maintain a steady stream of the benefits of stardom.

Ironically, the more fame a society produces, the more its creative vitality is likely to come from the nonfamous. Established stars, who by definition are the best known performers, will appear to lack in merit when, as most do, they turn conservative. Since the best known take the fewest chances, the illusion will be produced that culture is corrupt or declining. Yet creativity will remain vibrant in the initially hidden stratum of unknown and ambitious risk-takers. If new pools of risk-takers arise faster than they become famous, cultural innovation will continue to accelerate.

The best stars of the more fame-intensive society may not match the quality of the best stars of earlier times. Shakespeare, who was successful but not famous in his lifetime, did not have many laurels to rest upon. He wrote a steady stream of master-pieces once he reached a certain level. Modern stars, by con-trast, become conservative early on, precisely because they achieve fame so quickly. The more fame-intensive society will produce more stars, and arguably more total innovation, but each individual star may have a career of lower innovation, on average. The more crowded market brings fewer creative superstars, fewer Beethovens and Bachs. In sum, in a fame-intensive society, very many people try to be stars, most of them fail, a relatively large remainder succeed, the successful stars start off as innovative, and the established stars become conservative with relative rapidity.

Established stars may decline for another reason as well. The early receipt of fame, and therefore wealth, may weaken performers' drive to perfect their creations or develop innova-tions. In the contemporary world of rock and roll, successful performers become famous after one or two notable albums, sometimes within a year's time of entering the market. The British rock band Oasis achieved almost mythical status after only two albums, and were very popular even after the first one. Oasis members are now extremely wealthy, prestigious, and in high demand. On one hand their wealth supports their creative freedom, but on the other hand they may find it more difficult to summon up the drive and concentration to produce musical innovations. Indeed, their third album, released in 1997, does not measure up to the first two.

Economists might argue that Oasis members are simply deciding to enjoy leisure, and that no overall harm is associated with their decline. Yet an inefficiency remains. Oasis, like most creators of reproducible products, cannot internalize the full value of their output in the form of profits. Listeners gain from having Oasis "in the air," and Oasis cannot capture all of these benefits. Early fame and wealth, if they induce a decline in Oasis effort, worsen these market imperfections. Less fame would instead induce Oasis to invest more effort and energy in their products, which would counteract these initial distortions.

The measurement of performance that accompanies fame also limits risk-taking behavior. Individuals have the greatest latitude for taking risks when their behavior is not watched, monitored, and critically scrutinized. Performers kept on a short leash have less autonomy and fewer opportunities to express their vision in creative works. Performance measurement increases the cost of errors and therefore encourages behavior aimed merely at remaining in the market.

Improved measurement limits risk-taking in book and music markets. Most American stores now use electronic scanners, which allow book and record sales to be tallied and reported almost immediately. Although these electronic reporting systems increase the stores' profitability, increase the number of stores, and allow each store to carry more titles, they also involve a downside. Creators pay greater attention to producing immediate audience satisfaction, for fear of having their wares rapidly removed from the shelves on account of poor sales. More performers will explore the styles that please audiences immediately, and fewer will explore challenging and risky styles that require greater audience reaction time or education. Some authors even market new novels under pseudonyms to avoid being tagged with the poor sales records of their previous books.[14]

REPUTATIONAL COSTS FOR ALL

The costs of fame and excess visibility arise at local levels, not just nationally and internationally. Fear of gossip and negative reactions enforce conformity and conservative behavior, even when individuals prefer a more open modus operandi. Workplace norms discourage homosexuals from coming out of the closet; gay people might be better off if they did not care what fellow workers thought of them. The search for approbation and the fear of losing face may limit diversity and lead to excess conformity in outward behavior. The small town that relies on the personal reuptations of its citizens to produce public goods and a spirit of community also generates restrictive and controlling moralities. Everybody, not just celebrities, faces local constraints of reputation and must endure a "burden of fame," albeit with smaller groups of people.

Some commentators portray Japan as a society characterized by high degrees of visibility and lack of privacy. Japanese schoolchildren have little free time, workers and even managers rarely have private offices, residents of company housing find that their behavior is closely monitored, families question the neighbors of an individual before agreeing to an arranged marriage, Japanese walls are very thin, and in-laws typically exercise a high degree of influence over marriages. These mechanisms increase cooperativeness and tighten social norms, but they also impose onerous burdens. Individuals experience greater pressures for conformity, and find it harder to pursue and implement innovations.[15]

The quest for reputation produces negative effects in business as well. Consider the saying "Nobody ever got fired for buying IBM." Careerist managers may excessively mimic each other to avoid being blamed for mistakes. When one manager errs, superiors may assume that the manager exhibited poor judgment. But when several managers imitate each other's behavior, and (sometimes) end up making a common mistake, their superiors are more likely to assume that the world was too difficult to predict. The attempt to protect and extend reputation thus can stifle innovation. In a similar fashion, celebrity musicians may fear the consequences of trying out new styles, or their record companies may oppose their innovations. These individuals are reluctant to risk their reputational capital on untried approaches.[16]

FAME-SEEKING, FRAUD, AND OTHER EXCESSES

The Chicago School and free market traditions in economics typically treat reputation as a factor that encourages cooperative behavior and beneficial market outcomes. Yet desires for reputation often lead to fraud and falsification of information. Reputation is a double-edged sword, not an unambiguous force favoring cooperative behavior.[17]

Fame-seeking has caused information to be withheld rather than shared. Francis Crick and James Watson, winners of the Nobel Prize for discovering DNA, kept other scientists in the dark about their efforts, for fear that they would lose scientific priority. The search for superconductivity in the 1980s also developed into a competitive race rather than an information-sharing endeavor. Scientists from the time of Isaac Newton published their results in the form of anagrams, so that they could keep the scientific secret but subsequently prove their priority. The quest for fame makes scientists and other creators more secretive and less cooperative.[18]

The explorer Richard Byrd deliberately falsified his diaries by claiming that he had reached the North Pole when he had not. Soldiers, to win medals and honors, sometimes artificially manufacture situations where bravery is called for. In contrast, the truth often is told when individuals are unconcerned with their reputations. The truth-telling propensity of clowns, buffoons, jesters and others outside of mainstream society is a common theme in the plays of William Shakespeare. King Richard II is surrounded by flatterers who dare not speak the truth. Only Gaunt, a man on his deathbed with no further concern for his reputation, dares to tell the king that his kingdom is collapsing and his situation is hopeless.[19]

Individuals often behave more brutally, are unwilling to apologize, and are disinclined to accept a beneficial compromise when they are being watched by a group or crowd. They behave this way because they worry too much about the opinion of others. Presidents often feel that they must take tough military action to appear to be strong leaders. The youth gangs of Los Angeles and New York pressure their members to commit criminal acts, and the members comply, even though they might have chosen a more peaceful course of action on their own. Pride and status-seeking do not always bring out the best qualities in people.[20]

Parental approval or disapproval locks children into habits and characteristics acquired early. Even at advanced ages, most people have not shed the self-images molded by their parents, for better or worse. Almost every person is "famous" within his or her own family, and not always for the better.

Salespeople employ manipulative sales pitches to exploit the vulnerability of approval-seekers; Robert Cialdini refers to these individuals as "compliance professionals." Joe Girard, once renowned as the "world's greatest car salesman," sent his customers and would-be customers a card every month that merely said, "I like you," and mentioned Joe's name. Other salespeople promise their approval if the customer buys and threaten their disapproval if the customer does not buy. Customers who care about approbation are more vulnerable than others to external sales manipulation.[21]

Ironically, the infamous and the disgraced possess significant freedoms that more respectable citizens often lack. The Czech writer Jaroslav Hašek, in his satire *The Good Soldier Schweik*, noted that the inmates of a lunatic asylum have escaped reputational constraints: "the amount of liberty there is something that even the socialists have never dreamed of." In the eighteenth century, Bernard Mandeville, in *Fable of the Bees*, pointed out that whores were least likely to kill their babies following an illegitimate birth. Whores faced no additional negative reputational sanctions; the reputation of the whore was already so low that she lost no approbation by having an illegitimate child. Women in "proper families," by contrast, feared the stigma of illegitimacy. Many tried to hide their pregnancies and did away with the infant before anyone knew about the birth.[22]

BENTHAM'S AUTO-ICON PANOPTICON

Jeremy Bentham's essay *Auto-Icon* illustrates the dark side of a society obsessed with reputation. Bentham, who wanted to subject all human behavior to utilitarian manipulation, realized that control required observation. He sought to construct a society based on fame and reputation, even after death. That was his form of total observation.

Bentham's Panopticon, a model prison designated by the Greek term for "all seeing," provided the seed of the Auto-Icon idea. The Panopticon places all prisoners under perpetual observation. Cells are arranged in a polygon with the cells around the circumference and the warden seated in the middle, so that the prisoners can never hide their actions from the warden— "every motion of the limbs, and every muscle of the face [is] exposed to view."[23]

For Bentham, the Panopticon was not merely a plan for a prison. It was also a model for poorhouses, homes for wayward girls, orphanages, and, as many commentators have speculated, society itself. Bentham's detailed descriptions of the Panopticon sound like a portrait of a complete society rather than a mere prison. Prisoners even hold property rights and serve as residual claimants to the product of their labors. The Panopticon would have its own coinage, newspapers, almanacs, and maps. The Panopticon homes for paupers and children were intended to serve as fully self-sufficient, profit-making enterprises, while simultaneously supplying a full array of social services. Bentham stipulated that the Panopticon be built "near London," the "great seat of inspection." In his old age he wrote of the Panopticon as a "magnificent instrument with which I then dreamed of revolutionizing the world."[24]

The Panopticon makes all individuals visible to others in every nook and cranny of their lives. The Panopticon was no fleeting idea; it constituted the center of Bentham's life and thought. He devoted twenty-three years of his life to lobbying for construction of a Panopticon and endured bankruptcy during the struggle. The plan never came to fruition, even though Parliament passed a special act authorizing construction of a Panopticon.[25]

The Auto-Icon proposal, formulated later in Bentham's life, placed even the dead under scrutiny, thereby extending the reach of fame, and thus control, beyond the grave. Writing in all seriousness, Bentham proposes that we take the bodies of the dead, treat them and dry them out to prevent spoilage, and put them on public display. Either the bodies or just the heads could be placed in churches, on town gates, or in homes and public places. "If a country gentleman had rows of trees leading to his dwelling, the Auto-Icons of his family might alternate with the trees," Bentham wrote.[26]

We almost believe that Bentham is joking when we read passages like the following: "Would the sight,—the constant sight of the dead be too melancholy,—too saddening to the living? A curtain or sliding screen provides a remedy." Yet we know that Bentham is entirely serious. He had his own body preserved, stuffed, and placed in the University College of London, where it sits to this very day.[27]

The Auto-Icons will keep the dead ever in the mind of the living. Individuals will take the interests of posterity into account, since they are always being observed by posterity. Our blunders and magnificent deeds will not soon be forgotten. The Panopticon proposal was based on the premise that observation is essential to control, and the Auto-Icon plan takes observation one step further. The full control of individuals involves watching them for as long as possible. The Panopticon had left open one means of escape—death—from the observation of the jailer, but the Auto-Icon scheme attempts to plug this loophole. (The manuscript "Auto-Icon," which was not published in Bentham's lifetime, serves as a kind of paper Auto-Icon for Bentham, as do his other works.)

Bentham calls for the construction of an Auto-Icon Temple of Fame, to honor truly notable individuals. Other Auto-Icons, however, will be reproached for their bad deeds. Bentham also called for special days of celebration and religious observation during which people would pay special attention to the Auto-Icons in their midst. He writes that Prime Minister William Pitt would not have burdened the British Empire with so much debt had the Auto-Icon plan been in operation.[28]

The Auto-Icon plan seeks to control the living rather than to honor the dead for their own sake; Bentham even gives his scheme the subtitle "Farther Uses of the Dead to the Living." To achieve these beneficial ends, the scrutiny of the dead must never cease: "New motives will thus be brought into the field of thought and action,—motives both moral and political. What will be said of my Auto-Icon hereafter? The good report obtained by good conduct will attach to the man after death,— he will not be consigned to oblivion,—he must anticipate the judgment of his fellow men. If the judgment is unfavourable, he may be exposed with his head reversed. This would be the Auto-Icon purgatory; and should opinion change, the head might be set upright."[29]

THE BURDENS OF FAME

Many of the costs of fame fall upon the famous. Extreme levels of visibility do not always have favorable effects on the human psyche. Fame can be a burden, a dangerous addiction, and a source of excess hubris. Despite its considerable benefits, fame is also a trap.

Given how many people seek fame ardently, it may at first glance seem odd to argue that fame makes stars worse off. To paraphrase Oscar Wilde, perhaps the only thing worse than being famous is not being famous. Nonetheless, most stars have conflicting and unresolved feelings about their fame. Contrary to what a narrow economic framework would suggest, stars benefit from fame less than their ardent fame-seeking efforts seem to indicate. Fame changes individuals, their preferences, and their goals. We cannot evaluate a fame-intensive society without pondering the nature of the good life and asking whether fame delivers what it promises.

The benefits of fame are obvious. The famous usually enjoy riches, experience strong feelings of triumph, and have an easy time attracting sexual partners and spouses. Cheering crowds give stars a sense of power and a feeling of adulation that most people can barely imagine. Top stars have the world at their fingertips. Yet Marilyn Monroe remarked that fame "is not what fulfills you . . . When you're famous, every weakness is exaggerated."[30]

A recurring tradition in the history of ideas stresses the danger of fame to the star. The Stoics, many Christian theologians, Petrarch, Dante, Milton, and Arthur Schopenhauer all questioned whether fame should be treated as an ordinary object of desire, rather than as a burden, addiction, or illusion. Homer and the Greeks also recognized that the famous do not always benefit from their renown. In the *Iliad* Achilles is told that a short life is the price of his glory, and he is filled with bitterness at this exchange. In book 11 of the *Odyssey* Achilles sits remorseful in the underworld, despite the fame he had achieved. He says he would rather live on earth as a poor farm hand than "lord it over all the exhausted dead." Greek heroes produce the glory of the song, but they suffer early death from challenging the gods, and and are condemned to a gloomy and lifeless existence in the underworld. An old Jewish proverb says, "If you wish to live long, don't become famous."[31]

Shakespeare stressed the ambivalence, unhappiness, and impotency of kings and leaders. Henry V is a fame-seeker par excellence, but dies an early death, and plunges England into a bloody war with France. Coriolanus, who is obsessed with fame-seeking, brings death to himself and political chaos to Rome. Many Shakespearean rulers relinquish their thrones or bring on premature death. Hamlet's indecisiveness and unwillingness to seize power leads to his demise; King Lear gives up his throne prematurely, despite sensing his subsequent vulnerability; Macbeth does little to fend off his impending destruction; and Antony, wooing Cleopatra, neglects the duties of state to pursue sensual pleasures. In the opening scene of Henry VI, Part I, Shakespeare refers to "King Henry the Fifth, too famous to live long!"[32]

The available evidence offers a mixed answer to whether fame lowers life expectancy. One sample of a hundred very famous people, taken from Jib Fowles's book *Starstruck,* indicates that the very famous have shorter lives than other people. Fowles also finds that stars face higher death rates from cirrhosis (often a sign of alcoholism), homicide, kidney disease, accidents, ulcers, and suicides (the rate is more than three times higher for celebrities). The many premature deaths of rock stars are well known.[33]

This evidence must be interpreted with caution. For larger samples of stars I have not been able to find systematic effects on life expectancy; perhaps the costs of fame plague only the very famous. Furthermore, we cannot easily distinguish cause from effect. Nervous, erratic, and unstable personalities might be more likely to win fame in the first place, perhaps because of greater creativity or greater propensities to take risks. Finally, premature death may cause or augment an individual's fame (see Chapter 2), reversing the chain of cause and effect. Regardless of the effects on life expectancy, however, the psychological costs of fame are borne out by anecdotal evidence and the accounts of the stars themselves.

Illusions and Delusions

Many celebrities sour on fame as their careers progress. The rock star Pat Benatar told an interviewer that she was desperate to become famous at the age of twenty-two, indifferent at twenty-six, and by the age of twenty-eight had come to detest fame. The famous face higher expectations, greater demands on their time, and greater pressures to succeed, given the large sums of money at stake. Many people underestimate these costs when they start to seek fame. The television actor Jason Priestley said, "You never think about the price of fame when you start out. You're far too busy trying to work. All of a sudden you find yourself a working actor and six months later you've got *Hard Copy* camped out on your doorstep." And the actor Michael Maloney said that "anyone who craves fame is not aware of the consequences."[34]

The search for fame derives in part from personal insecurities. Both Blaise Pascal and Adam Smith argued that individuals look to others for approval when they are uncertain about the quality of their decisions and contributions. According to Pascal, if someone tells us that we have a headache when we do not, we are not upset. We know that the opinion has no merit. If someone criticizes us and tells us that an opinion of ours is wrong, however, we are greatly disturbed. We cannot be certain that our opinion is correct, and the expressed disapproval makes us nervous. Approbation has its greatest force when insecurity is most prominent.[35]

Adam Smith compared poets and mathematicians. The quality of poetry, he thought, is difficult to judge, which makes poets

The Dark Side of Fame

insecure about their work. They seek favor with great ardor, and divide themselves into cabals and factions. Mathematicians, by contrast, have greater assurance about the quality of their work, even when they receive little or no public recognition. Since right and wrong answers usually can be proven, time will validate the merit of their contributions. According to Smith, mathematicians enter into less intrigue than do poets, and they reject participation in factions and cabals.[36]

To the extent that fame-seeking is based in personal insecurity, the attainment of fame will not eradicate performers' underlying feelings of inadequacy. The receipt of approval often *feeds* upon insecurities. It nourishes and magnifies fears, rather than alleviating them. The fame-seeker is trying to fill a personal void by addressing symptoms rather than causes, by looking for external approval instead of internal self-respect. The magnification and intensification of fame brought by modernity can heighten these tendencies and spread them to larger numbers of people. Hegel viewed the attainment of recognition as alienating for both parties, since it elevates the status of one human being over another.[37]

One burden of fame is the admiration itself. The renowned often find fame repugnant when they ponder its meaning, as Andy Warhol once said. Fans treat celebrities as symbols or as surrogates, not as actual individuals. Most people would feel successful if they breakfasted with the President, gave a luncheon speech to the Trilateral Commission, played a pick-up game with Grant Hill in the afternoon, and jammed with the Rolling Stones at night. People take the fame of others as a measure of their self-aggrandizement and they seek to consume the fame of celebrities as a way of demonstrating power. Each time a famous person receives attention, he or she is the victim of a power play on the part of the attention-giver. Like vampires, fans and attention-givers feast upon the fame of others for their own selfish reasons.[38]

Stars have a difficult time making and keeping true friends. The potential friend of the star cannot easily demonstrate the sincerity of his or her motives. In turn, the star holds the superior position and cannot easily negotiate a position of parity. For these reasons, movie stars tend to marry each other, and the super-rich tend to befriend other members of the super- rich. When famous or powerful people do have close friends of non-comparable status, these friends tend to come from their childhoods or earlier lives, before they attained fame or power .

Fame gives celebrities an exaggerated sense of their self-importance and leads them into a mix of hyperbole, lies, and delusions. The fashion designer Valentino told NBC that Princess Diana's death was the "most emotional moment of my life." The actress Geena Davis complained when physicist Stephen Hawking did not respond to her letter to him explaining how he might rebut the Heisenberg Uncertainty Principle.[39]

Research by cognitive psychologists suggests that people overestimate their chance of becoming famous. A survey of a wide sample of sociologists asked them how much future influence they expected to wield and how much professional fame they expected to achieve. Almost half of the 198 polled said they expected to stand among the top 10 leaders in their field. More than half expected that their writings would continue to be read after their careers had ended. These claims were then subjected to a "reality test." The pollster, Frank Westie, compared the sociologists' claims with the achievements of the past presidents of the American Sociological Society, a group deliberately selected for prestige; most of the 198 sociologists he polled will never reach that level of achievement. Yet few sociologists from the list of past presidents had achieved lasting fame, even among their peers. The work of 19 of these 63 past presidents was unknown to more than 50 percent of the polled sample of sociologists. The work of 25 past presidents was unknown to more than half of the younger sociologists polled. Most sociologists appear to have "unrealistically high" expectations of professional immortality.[40]

Both Stoic and Christian critiques of fame-seeking argued that fame appears more valuable *ex ante* than it turns out to be *ex post*. Boethius argued that fame is no benefit at all. Even the greatest fame is extremely limited through time and space, compared with the size and history of the universe, or compared with the mind of God. In Boethius' view, humans pursue fame because they attach excess importance to their immediate surroundings and circumstances.[41]

The narrator of Dante's *Divine Comedy*, using similar arguments, presented fame as fleeting and transitory, even though it is widely sought:

O empty glory of human endeavour!
How little time the green remains on top,
Unless the age that follows is a dull one!

Cimabue thought he held the field
In painting, and now the cry is for Giotto,
So that the other's fame is now obscured . . .

Earthy fame is nothing but a breath of wind,
Which first blows one way and then blows another,
And brings a fresh name from each fresh direction.

What greater name will you have, if you are old
When you put aside your flesh, than if you had died
Before you had given up baby-talk and rattles,

Once a thousand years have passed? And that is a shorter
Space to the eternal than the flash of an eyelid
To the circle which turns in the heavens most slowly.[42]

Similar arguments run throughout Renaissance poetry. Chaucer's *House of Fame* emphasized the transitory nature of earthly reputation. Drawing upon metaphors from the Bible, Boccaccio wrote of fame as a grass that eventually turns dry and brown, even if the world endures. Petrarch, in his *Triumphs*, wrote of the triumph of time over fame. "Your fame is nothing more than a sunlit day, / Or a doubtful winter: clouds may end it all. / Great length of time is poisonous to great names." The final stanza of the section of the poem on fame described fame not as a second life, but rather as a second death, since fame must eventually dwindle. John Milton, in his poems *Paradise Lost, Paradise Regained,* and *Lycidas,* also portrayed fame as transient and of illusory appeal.[43]

Shakespeare's Falstaff supported the Stoic view that reputation confers no real benefit:

Honor pricks me on. Yea, but how if honor prick me off when I come on? How then? Can honor set to a leg? No. Honor hath no skill in surgery, then? No. What is honor? A word. What is in that word "honor"? What is that "honor"? Air. A trim reckon-ing. Who hath it? He that died o' Wednesday. Doth he feel it? No. Doth he hear it? No. 'Tis insensible, then? Yea, to the dead. But will [it] not live with the living? No. Why? Detraction will not suffer

The Dark Side of Fame

it. Therefore, I'll none of it. Honor is a mere scutcheon. And so ends my catechism.[44]

Addiction

Saint Augustine remarked that even the relatively virtuous usually are keen for external recognition and cannot resist the temptations of earthly praise. Tacitus noted that "the lust of fame is the last that a wise man shakes off." Montaigne claimed that we cannot remove the desire for recognition from ourselves, no matter how hard we try. Even the Stoics, according to Montaigne, never ceased to seek external recognition. Cicero notes that even those who scorn fame, and who write polemics against it, do not hesitate to attach their name to their works.[45]

Many of the celebrities interviewed by Joey Berlin for his study of the psychology of the modern celebrity refer to fame as toxic, intoxicating, and addictive. Even those who are aware of the costs of fame may not be able to resist the material, sexual, and approbational rewards that accompany renown. The receipt of fame induces people to seek more and more external recognition, even if fame does not benefit them in the long run. They become addicted to the praise of others, and they go to ever greater trouble to seek that reward and to fend off criticism. Fame addicts may be increasingly bound to public acclaim and decreasingly unable to enjoy other pleasures in life. Adam Smith, in *Theory of Moral Sentiments,* wrote, "To those who have been accustomed to the possession, or even to the hope of public admiration, all other pleasures sicken and decay."[46]

One commentator, Drew Brown, Jr., once said about Muhammed Ali: "Ali was a junkie . . . He needed to see his name in lights; he had to hear the crowd. There's only one sport in the world where they say, 'And in this corner, the undisputed heavyweight champion of the world, Muhammad Ali.' That's addictive; everything always revolving around you, everyone telling you you're the greatest. Ali never messed with drugs, but he was a junkie for fame" This quest for ongoing approval motivated Ali to continue fighting, even though he sustained serious damage to his motor skills.[47]

Fans and critics implicitly understand the plight of the famous and try to manipulate them. Special interest groups mobilize public sentiment to pressure political leaders. Few politicians wish to be viewed as bad leaders or as heartless or uncaring. Fans of stars will turn into enemies if the star does not make public appearances and sign autographs. Sports fans boo stars who occasionally sit out of a game to rest. The famous confront an active, manipulative public that seeks to control them through the strategic use of praise and blame.

Muhammed Ali's promoters encouraged him to take on more fights, despite the pounding his brain was taking. Mary Boone, a New York gallery dealer, described her relations with the painters she exhibited and promoted: "Get them into debt. What you always want to do as an art dealer is to get the artist to have expensive tastes. Get them to buy lots of houses, get them to have expensive habits and girlfriends, and expensive wives. That's what I love. I really encourage it. That's what really drives them to produce." Profit-seeking intermediaries encourage and stimulate the addictions of stars.[48]

Adaptive preferences further raise the costs of addictive fame-seeking. Sustainable increases in happiness often require continual improvements in one's circumstances. Immediately upon being elected President and assuming office, the candidate experiences a great thrill and a rush of fame and power. Over time, however, the immediate impact wears off and the Presidency becomes part of the person's daily expectations. Further victories and achievements are required to sustain the giddiness of the initial moment. Bill Clinton, who was disappointed by the failure of his health plan, could not just fall back upon his previous laurels of being President, governor of Arkansas, or Rhodes Scholar. Even the most talented individuals often end up frustrated because after a certain point further victories become difficult to attain. Stars, who are often motivated by an initial need to be loved, end up in arenas where hostility and eventual rejection are almost certain.

Changes in our circumstances often have a greater influence on our happiness than the circumstances themselves. Our expectations tend to adjust to whatever level of comfort we have achieved, thereby causing us to want more. People who win the lottery, for instance, often are not happier than before for long, once their expectations adjust to the new level of wealth. By the same token, people who suffer great misfortunes, such as becoming permanently handicapped because of an accident, often report several years later that their level of happiness has not decreased.[49]

Achieving fame creates a problem similar to the well-known golden handcuffs syndrome. Renowned people enjoy high absolute rewards but face strong constraints. (Analogously, in the golden handcuffs problem, employees with high salaries find it difficult to leave their jobs.) The renowned cannot do as they please without losing their fame or incurring scorn and wrath. The very fame of an individual represents the subordination of that person to the will of the masses; individuals become famous only through being controlled. Famous celebrities are poorly insulated from the opinion of the public, and they face high reputational costs for doing what they please.

If the increase in well-being is largely illusory in the long term, once preferences and expectations have adjusted, the famous are trapped in the worst of all possible worlds. Their fame brings little benefit, while they are imprisoned by their need to preserve their reputation.[50]

Regard for others, or the views of others, often proves a disadvantage in strategic situations and makes an person prone to manipulation. People who are known to care about their reputations, for instance, may be expected to carry more than their share of a collective burden, or they may end up worrying about how others regard them. People who can cultivate indifference toward public opinion may achieve objectives at lower personal cost. As Spinoza wrote, "Fame has the further drawback that it compels its votaries to order their lives according to the opinions of their fellow-men, shunning what they usually shun, and seeking what they usually seek."[51]

The Stoic critique of fame-seeking rested on a judgment about the quality of differing preferences. According to the Stoics, men should be self-sufficient and unmindful of the opinions of others. The perfect life is based on self-satisfaction and inner contentment, rather than on public recognition. Epictetus, for instance, believed that individuals attain personal bliss by ignoring the words of others and by perfecting their own wills. The true Stoic can learn to be happy with what he or she has, but the famous find this strategy especially difficult to implement, because they are trying to please their audiences.[52]

Many fame-seekers are doomed to have frustrated preferences. Joseph Addison wrote of fame-seeking as an addiction that produces no real satisfaction and that leads to a spiral of desire, corrupting the fame-seeker. Those who seek fame betray themselves and perform indecent acts. Fame-seekers recite their own praises, boast excessively, and ruin their characters by the pursuit of gain.

Fame-seeking is self-frustrating for another reason as well: fame-givers view the pursuit of fame as a character weakness. If fans and critics see that an individual is obsessed with fame, they are likely to withhold their approbation. Fans and critics are repelled by such people , and they do not wish to pander to their vanity. Addison wrote, "those are generally most unsuccessful in their Pursuit after Fame, who are most desirous of obtaining it. It is *Sallust's* remark upon *Cato,* that the less he coveted Glory the more he acquired it." Along similar lines, George McKenzie described fame as a "coy maid . . . that it courts most those who seem most to undervalue it."[53]

7 Lessons for the Future

Robert Ashley, writing in the late sixteenth century, told his readers:

> For by honour are vertues kindled and incouraged, by honour are vices eschewed, by honour ignoraunce, error and folly, sloth and sluggishnes, hatred and fear, shame and ignoraunce, and all evill affeccions are alayed, Calmed, and quieted, by honour are Citties kept, famelies preserved, the society of men quietly and peaceably continued, the common wealth defended, dominions enlarged, the warrs well followed, learning cherished, and all artes mainteyened. To conclude, without honour no one thing can be well administred or worthely effected. Take honour out of vertuous accions you take away all delight of the mind and easines of accion. Magnanimitie will perish, fortitude, moderacion, and decencie will decay, and observaunce of lawes and lawes themselves wilbe neglected, offyces of honour despised, magistrates contemned, discordes arise amongst

Cittizens, and every one dare to do each foule and wicked deed.[1]

Eighteenth-century economists were preoccupied with these issues, but since that time the economics of approbation has mostly existed as an underground tradition. In seeking to resurrect these inquiries, I have asked whether the modern world of fame and celebrity brings benefits or whether it corrupts our society, culture, and polity.

I have been suggesting a shift of the intellectual balance toward a relatively favorable account of modern fame-seeking, renown, and celebrity. Building on the Scottish Enlightenment tradition of Smith and Hume, we can reinterpret the "corruptions" identified by Plato and by the critics of modern culture. The contemporary world of fame is a highly effective means for mobilizing the large-scale production of renown and supporting the exchange of praise for performance. Modernity brings forth a diverse and plentiful array of achievements in science, business, and the arts, in part through greasing the wheels of approbational exchange.

These processes will not grant recognition and acclaim in proportion to worth. The application of twentieth-century microeconomics to eighteenth-century questions yields the surprising result that a successful society—defined in terms of science, business, politics, and the creative arts—is bound to separate fame from merit to a large degree.

False beliefs can be very useful for society, as I have stressed throughout this book. We produce ideas and standards of achievement to serve many purposes, not just to reflect the truth. Of course many people do not see through the confusion of fame—they believe that Madonna is better than Mozart—

but that is the price we pay for the diverse outputs that fame-seeking elicits. We cannot have great intellectual and cultural diversity without simultaneously enduring an oversimplified popular culture.

Many of the triumphs of contemporary culture spring from its production of immense quantities of fame, but at the same time many of its failures can be traced to the limits of fame and to imperfections in fame markets. Fame incentives—relatively blunt instruments in most cases—entail complex and contradictory effects by their very nature. Even when modern fame institutions are good for most of society, they are often bad for the famous and for the creativity of the famous, as I have already pointed out.

Some of the more specific lessons to be learned from this investigation of the mechanisms of fame can be divided into three groups: lessons for policy, lessons for morality, and lessons for political philosophy.

POLICY

Given the various imperfections of fame markets, it is possible in principle for government intervention to improve our culture and our polity. I have argued that we cannot interpret fame markets as a first-best, welfare-maximizing competitive equilibrium. The theorems of economics then imply that a better outcome must exist.

Nonetheless, as a practical matter most government fine-tunings of the fame market are unlikely to succeed. We should be reluctant to restrict or tax commercialization per se. We would not, for instance, choose a lower rather than a higher rate of economic growth. Yet without restricting commercialization, it is difficult to reign in the central tendencies discussed in this book. In a world with private enterprise and free speech, commercial forces *will* rule the production of fame and to an increasing degree, as the technologies of electronic reproduction become more powerful.

Many of the market failures I have discussed are subtle and not easily susceptible to corrective interventions. Take, for instance, the argument, put forth in Chapter 2, that the coordination of large numbers of fans requires heroes to be excessively obvious and simplistic, in order to become "focal." How might we design an intervention to overcome this problem? Should the government be assigned the task of identifying the underappreciated, sophisticated heroes and subsidizing their fame? It is difficult to believe that such a foray into the world of ideas is likely to succeed, especially when we consider the "public choice" aspects of the problem. Governments will be inclined to promote heroes to serve political agendas, rather than to focus everyone's attention on Charles Ives and William Faulkner.

Or take the argument that markets produce the most profitable stars, rather than the set of stars that fans value most highly. A program of taxes and subsidies to remedy this distortion is again unlikely to succeed, given the information and governmental discretion it would require. The necessary remedies also would run afoul of the principle of equal taxation under the law and arguably would violate the First Amendment.

More plausibly, the government could, as a counterweight to commercialized fame production, subsidize high culture, public television, and other alternative sources of information about the famous or would-be famous. This book is not the place for a systematic policy analysis of these proposals, which have merits and demerits apart from their effects on fame. The previous chapters nonetheless suggest that *less* is at stake in these policy issues than is commonly supposed. The United States has an eight trillion dollar economy, large chunks of which are focused on the commercial production of fame. For better or worse, marginal policy changes are unlikely to bring fundamental reform in the nature of these fame markets.[2]

Similar points apply to debates about educational policy. Should schoolchildren be taught that Thomas Jefferson was a libertarian hero or a roguish slaveholder? Should history or computer science receive more attention in the junior high curriculum? Should Pocahontas or Betsy Ross be considered the great American heroine? Regardless of our views on these issues, the analysis of this book suggests that less is at stake than is commonly supposed. The forces of commercial fame—Michael Jordan on the Wheaties box—will in any case play a dominant role in creating the popular social climate.

If any policy lesson can be drawn, we should hold the American system of tax deductions for charitable deductions in high regard. Moving toward a fully flat tax system would damage the production of long-run fame and decrease the supply of public goods. The production of long-term honor in America relies, in part, on decentralized charitable giving and endowments. Art museums, wings of hospitals, and libraries, among other public goods, have been named after wealthy benefactors. At smaller scales, a disproportionate percentage of charitable contributions are just above the level needed to achieve recognition on a plaque or on a list of prominent donors. The use of our tax system to subsidize these contributions has had favorable effects on the world of fame and on our polity more generally.[3]

MORALITY

While I have defended the practicality of the modern world of fame and celebrity, I have not asked whether it is moral to partake in fame-seeking and fame production. Yet throughout the centuries this question has preoccupied most theorists of fame. Plato's critique has already been discussed. Christian thinkers generally frowned on fame-seeking, which they regarded as a challenge to the power of God. Kant and Habermas draw upon the Platonic tradition.

I suggest that we take alternative philosophical approaches to this question. Roman thought was sympathetic to the competitive production of rhetoric, as were Aristotle and many of the Greek Sophists. The writers of the Scottish Enlightenment, such as Adam Smith and David Hume, took a pragmatic point of view. They recognized the practical benefits of "corrupt" speech and competitive rhetoric, rather than erecting a Platonic utopia as a moral standard. As Smith and Hume acknowledged, human nature has a significant selfish, narrow-minded, and biased component, but the quest for approbation nonetheless produces public goods through invisible hand mechanisms, through which self-seeking behavior acts in the public interest. To the extent that moral theory places weight on good consequences, we should hold morally relaxed attitudes toward fame-seeking, rather than condemning it.

Ironically, a fame-intensive society satisfies the demands of distributive justice more than is commonly recognized. Both critics and defenders of capitalism fail to perceive who really benefits from fame. It is often alleged that in a market economy the rich exploit the poor, but in the case of fame the opposite is more likely to occur. Fans, who tend to be poor, exploit their stars, who tend to be rich. The fans receive a performance, but the stars often end up miserable. They lose themselves by pursuing the adoration of the masses. It is the star who is alienated under capitalism, not necessarily the worker.

Many right-wing commentators overrate the lot of the famous as well. Contra Ayn Rand, the quest for creative excellence does not necessarily generate the highest fulfillment of selfish rationality. The pressures of celebrity, combined with the intensifying forces of a market economy, prevent many well-known people from achieving a satisfying balance, or "golden mean," in their lives. Rand herself set up a cult and became addicted to the adulations of her followers and groupies.

A further irony is that the least ardent fans may benefit most from the world of stardom. Just as many stars are victimized by fame, the fans who dedicate their lives to following and feting stars often remain unfulfilled. Fandom, in its most severe forms, is as an escape, an unhealthy obsession, and an unsatisfying pursuit. There is something crass about fandom that repels most thoughtful and intelligent observers.

Although the modern world of fame does not create fan personality disorders, and in many cases channels them in relatively harmless directions, it does intensify fan pathologies and make it easier to manifest them. In that regard, the modern world of fame is dangerously seductive for the potentially obsessive follower.

In contrast, casual listeners can enjoy, say, a Rolling Stones concert or album without having to exert great effort or direct their psyche in an unrewarding, obsessive fashion. The casual fans hitch a free ride on the efforts of the more ardent fans, reaping the benefits of fandom without incurring many of the costs. The quiet, undemonstrative person—albeit with some wealth and a taste for vicarious excitement—benefits most clearly from the modern world of fame.

POLITICAL PHILOSOPHY

Finally, the modern world of fame suggests new standards for evaluating our polity. It is now well known that the commercialization of fame makes political culture appear degraded. Modern politics emphasizes images, rumor, negative campaigning, and a circus-like, mass media atmosphere. Leaders lose their stature and become another set of celebrities. We talk about them and use them for entertainment. Yet contrary to the views of many critics, these developments are by no means wholly negative.

Commercial society has brought the taming of fame to politics. By its nature, politics remains coercive, and political fame is ultimately based on the ability to wield power effectively, no matter how beneficial or peaceful the final end may be. Politicians, however, have been forced to compete on the same terms as entertainers do—they must appeal to the public for support. Voters and other external forces, such as the media, have more control over politicians than ever before. Famous politicians are kept on a short leash, most of all by the media.

Although it is harder to install bold and innovative visionaries in political positions than it used to be, the danger of political abuse and very bad outcomes is smaller as well. The same forces that prevent America from generating another Franklin Roosevelt or Britain another Winston Churchill also limit demagoguery and power. All successful political orders must incur costs of some kind to suppress political risk-taking.

Modern fame therefore offers an alternative solution to the Hobbesian problem of political order. Hobbes believed that mutual fear, not fame-seeking, held society together. He associated glory-seekers with the desire for conquest and domination, and more generally, he believed that the quest for fame was a zero- or negative-sum game. Hobbes's answer was Leviathan. He saw a strong absolutist state as necessary to instill fear in people and inhibit their natural proclivities to seek status at each other's expense.[4]

Hobbes did not, however, solve the problem of political glory-seeking. The absolute power of sovereigns means that they can engage in brutal glory-seeking at public expense. Furthermore, very strong states offer a great potential prize to would-be glory-seekers, thus stirring quests for fame and power. Once in office glory-seekers must brutally suppress political opposition to keep power, giving rise to the precise problems— conflict and political risk-taking—that Hobbes sought to avoid. In essence, the Hobbesian recipe fails through excess centralization. Hobbes's own description of the sovereign as "the Fountain of Honour" points to the problem. The stronger the power of a state, the greater the returns from capturing control of that state. An absolutist state is the ultimate winner-take-all prize in a fame contest, to the detriment of political order.[5]

Fame and media scrutiny achieve the Hobbesian result of risk suppression, but without creating political instability. The burdens of fame provide a new means of limiting political leaders, a means overlooked by Hobbes and subsequent classical liberal commentators. The separation of fame and merit is part of the price we pay for modern democracy, which relies heavily on the media to monitor our leaders.

Many commentators, especially from those with left-wing or communitarian views, look to the quality of public discourse to secure political order and justice. I regard this as a utopian hope.

A fame-intensive society—a free and commercial society—cannot effectively regulate its state through the quality of public discourse. The very nature of commercial fame corrupts that discourse and creates a world of illusion and make-believe.

The resulting degradation in political culture goes along with an apparent decline in market culture, as we hear from many neo-conservatives and neo-Marxists. Modern commentators often criticize politics and citizenries for their low standards and their ignorance. In reality they are observing the consequences of a culture that is based on scrutiny of the famous and driven by the quest for profits.

Many of the cultural and political dilemmas of our time arise from this scrutiny. The quest for fame calls forth a vast and diverse array of skillful performances in culture, business, science, and many other areas, all achieved at relatively low cost. Modernity produces a social ideology based on individualism, self-fulfillment, and entertainment, the last often coming in forms involving simulated violence. Mores are relatively loose and shame has little power, as discussed in Chapter 6. Politics is based on media coverage and the promotion of images. Governments are very large by the standards of earlier times and they wield considerable power, yet they are held closely in thrall to the wishes of voters through the media. Politics is full of dishonest yet constrained political scoundrels. Such is the moral and political package brought by the modern commercialization of fame. The fate of our polity depends on whether this environment can allow liberty, prosperity, and culture to continue their growth.

Notes · References ·
Acknowledgments · Index

Notes

1 THE INTENSITY OF FAME IN MODERN SOCIETY

1. Fowles (1992, p. 44).

2. See Merton (1973, chap. 14, pp. 287–289, 293, and p. 335) and Stephan and Levin (1992, pp. 18–20).

3. John Adams (1851 [1790], p. 238 and passim) argued that even riches are desired for the recognition they bring. Furthermore, he attributed intellectual pursuits not to the love of knowledge, but to the love of reputation and recognition. Adams claims that if a Robinson Crusoe never expected to rejoin civilization, he would not read books, even if he held the library of Alexandria on his island (1851 [1790], p. 240). This theme also surfaces in the writings of Blaise Pascal.

Note that desires for recognition extend even to anonymous creators. The anonymous author of the recent bestseller *Primary Colors* (later revealed as Joe Klein of *Newsweek*) probably took great delight in the book's success and the praise it received. The author cared about his vicarious reputation, and was pleased to read the positive reviews, even though the praise was not directed to him by name. Similarly, war heroes take pride in the general respect shown to patriotism and heroism, even when few members of the public are aware of their particular deeds of heroism. Alumni and alumnae are pleased when they hear their alma mater praised, even if the speaker does not know that the listener attended that university.

In other cases, an honor does not have to be awarded at all. It suffices if the individual knows that the action *would have been honored* had the great deed come to light. Many war heroes choose license plates which indicate that they have won the Purple Heart or Congressional Medal of Honor. These people desire recognition from other drivers and perhaps from neighbors. Yet much of the honor received is abstract. The person's neighbors may learn that he or she is a war hero, but other drivers on the road do not have much information. They see the make of car and the back of somebody's head and conclude that this head probably belongs to a war hero. The other drivers merely see that *someone* is a war hero. This abstract form of recognition apparently gives satisfaction to the war hero, even if the other drivers never know whom they are looking at. See Smith (1981 [1759], p. 116).

4. For the Chapman quote, see Shales (1991, p. D1).

5. See Smith (1981 [1759], p. 57) and Hume (1966 [1777], p. 114). See also Pascal (1995, pp. 151–152). There are several overviews of thought on fame: Levy (1992) treats the Greeks and many Enlightenment writers; Lida de Malkiel (1983) covers antiquity through the Spanish Middle Ages; Koonce (1966) examines the early Christian tradition; Elton (n.d.) treats some Renaissance writers; Watson (1960) focuses on the Renaissance and Shakespeare; Jones (1960) studies honor in German literature, Lovejoy (1961) covers the Enlightenment and the seventeenth century; Crocker (1959, chap. 11) considers French thought; Tillotson (1966) examines British literary thought; Adair (1974) considers the Founding Fathers; Boitani (1984) covers the period up through Chaucer; Kojève (1969) discusses Hegel and recognition.

Robert H. Frank, who has studied status-seeking (1985) and winner-take-all "superstar" markets (the latter with Philip J. Cook, 1995), has done the most to bring fame and approbation to the attention of economists. David Levy (1992) asks the seminal question for an economics of approbation—what is the opportunity cost of praise? I draw other building blocks from a variety of social scientists, including George

Akerlof, Pierre Bourdieu, Leo Braudy, Geoffrey Brennan and Philip Pettit, Francis Fukuyama, William J. Goode, Jürgen Habermas, Albert O. Hirschman, Leo Katz, Timur Kuran, Richard Posner, and Thomas Schelling. Most economic models do not consider an expressive dimension at all. Deirdre McCloskey (1994, p. 82) wrote, "Speaking Man has never figured much in economics, even among institutional economists." Even McCloskey has focused on the rhetoric of economics rather than on the economics of rhetoric.

Outside the rational-choice tradition, William J. Goode (1978) treats the sociology of fame. Leo Braudy (1986) offers a history of the concept of renown from antiquity through the present day. David Lowenthal (1985) analyzes how societies produce pictures and memories of their pasts. Pierre Bourdieu (1993) has emphasized the production of "symbolic capital" in markets, especially in cultural markets. Diego Gambetta (1987) focuses on trust and reputation. In criticism, Alvin Kernan (1987) focuses on the fame incentives for literary production. Gary Taylor (1996) analyzes which cultural artifacts resonate in our memories and which do not. Lang and Lang (1990, pp. xv-xvi) offer an overview of the literature on collective memory, the development of literary and artistic reputations, and the production of fame through sports, among other topics. For an annotated bibliography of the historical research on collective memory, see Irwin-Zarecka (1994). Lowenthal (1996) offers an excellent survey of the issues involved with the preservation of heritage. On reputation more generally, see Posner (1981), Weigelt and Camerer (1988), Fombrun and Stanley (1990), and Mercer (1996), which survey the relevant literature from economics. Stewart (1994) surveys the concept of honor in anthropology.

6. Thurow (1997).

7. See Karger (1998).

8. On the friendship motive behind science fiction fandom, see Coulson (1994); on fanship and social status, see Bourdieu (1994).

9. See Ault (1981).

10. On Warhol, see Wilbon (1998); on Grant, see McCann (1996, p. 5).

11. Burek and Connor (1992, pp. 159, 207).

12. See Turner (1990).

13. See Vermoral and Vermoral (1985, p. 249). On Gould, see Ostwald (1997, p. 131). For the *Washington Post,* see "The Style Invitational" (1997). On celebrity death pools, see Weeks (1998).

14. For the epigram, see Swift (1958, p. 418), the essay entitled "Thoughts on Various Subjects."

15. See Strauss (1999).

16. See Fowles (1992, p. 182) and Vermoral and Vermoral (1985, pp. 11, 59, 80–82).

17. On Graceland, see Valhouli (1998, p. 58). On Yeltsin, see Thaler (1997, p. 186). On Jordan, see Johnson (1998).

18. On Halls of Fame, see Burns and Coffman (1976), Rein, Kotler, and Stoller (1987, p. 62), Soderberg, Washington, and Press (1977, p. xiv), Ferguson (1977), and Danilov (1997). The 3,000 estimate is from ABC-TV's *World News Tonight,* cited by Danilov (1997, p. 1).

19. Plato (1968, p. 290). For a detailed study of Plato's critique of the arts, see Janaway (1995). Plato's *Symposium* (1956) presented love as an alternative means of distributing praise, but even he admitted the impracticality of implementing this idea on a society-wide basis. On love, Socrates claimed, "if there were only some way of contriving that a State or an army should be made up of lovers and their loves, they would be the very best governors of their own city, abstaining from all dishonor, and emulating one another in honor." See Plato (1956, pp. 341–342).

20. See Mandeville (1988 [1735]).

21. On this reading of Plato, I am indebted to Prendergast (1986, pp. 12–13), who in turn draws upon Derrida (1981).

2 WHY FAME IS SEPARATED FROM MERIT

1. See Kuran (1995).

2. In contrast, when Wayne Newton sings in Las Vegas, the concert has little hope of attracting young fans, because of both the price and the content. Wayne Newton knows he will not attract the very young and he doesn't care much if they cannot afford his high ticket

prices. He is nearing the end of his career and is more likely to cash in on his current reputation than to invest in a future fan network.

3. In a different context, Tocqueville noted, "In a democratic nation such as are the people of America, in which ranks are confused and the whole of society forms one single mass composed of elements which are all analogous though not precisely similar, it is impossible ever to agree beforehand exactly what is allowed or forbidden by honor" (1969 [1835], p. 624).

4. For the Morrison quote, see Fowles (1992, p. 181). For the star's persona, see Harrington and Bielby (1995, p. 62).

5. I am indebted to Diego Gambetta for this point.

6. On Joyce, see Schickel (1985, p. 215).

7. See Raeburn (1984).

8. See Havill (1996).

9. Fowles (1992, p. 249).

10. On the marketing of dead celebrities, see Valhouli (1998).

11. On culture and differentiation, see Leibenstein (1976) and Bourdieu (1984).

12. See, for instance, Brown (1994, pp. 92–93).

13. On time consistency, see Schelling (1960) and Kydland and Prescott (1977).

14. For the quotation, see Weinstein (1991, pp. 137–138).

15. On this development within the music industry, see Strauss (1998). On this point in general I am indebted to discussions with Roger Trilling.

16. On negative blurbs, see Carvajal (1997).

17. Twitchell (1996) documents the ubiquity of advertising and social publicity in American life. For the figures, see Bogart (1995, pp. 69–72).

18. On the early history of payola, see Coase (1979) and Sanjek (1988, pp. 16–17). One study estimated 1985 music payola payments as in the range of $70–80 million; see Bogart (1995, pp. 228–229).

19. On the conflict of interest problems faced by critics, see English (1979) and Booth (1991). Twitchell (1996, pp. 117–120) documents the influence of advertisers on program content; see also Parenti (1993).

On newspapers, see English (1979, p. 101), and on the Golden Globe awards, see Waxman (1997).

20. See Habermas (1989, p. 167) on book clubs and how their evaluations bypass other fame-generating processes. Payola plays a prominent role in many other sectors as well. Investment advisors are paid to promote the purchase of stocks, Campbell's pays a slotting fee to be in the grocery store, and doctors pay referral fees to hospitals, to name a few other non–fame-related examples.

Even on the low-cost Internet, praise for sale and advertising are emerging in many forms. What is scarce on the Internet is not information or material, but context and evaluation. Even when text can be produced and posted at low cost, consumers cannot find the text at low cost, given the mass of other materials competing for fan attention. In fact, the lower the costs of posting on the Internet, the higher the costs for fans to find what they are looking for. The Web serves at least two fame-producing functions, each of which is subject to commercial incentives. First, Web browsers may help individuals find information about topics and stars from other media, such as television or the world of music. In this regard the Internet merely supports and magnifies other, predominantly commercial, means of producing fame. Second, Web browsers may in the future serve as a fame-generating technology. Sophisticated browsers, perhaps customized, will direct fan attention to the Web sites of new topics, new performers, and so on, thus serving as editors. If we extrapolate from current practices, these Web browsers will be given away for free, and they will finance their operation through the sale of advertising. Given the relative ease of copying software, and thus the difficulties of charging directly for its use, the growth of the Web may increase the prevalence of advertising in Western culture. The Internet cannot escape basic economic tradeoffs and may disappoint the anticommercial ideals of early cyberculture proponents. Whether Web advertising will prove profitable remains an open question. Subscription finance therefore remains a possible alternative. See Reid (1997, p. 274) on the implications of customized publishing and customized search services.

21. For the Berry story, see DeWitt (1985, pp. 25, 82).

22. On Greenberg, see English (1979, p. 98).

23. On the etchers, see Lang and Lang (1988). In the art market, note the differential treatment of prints and paintings. Prints, which are issued in multiple copies and sold to a wide range of buyers for considerably less than paintings, produce a less exclusive reputational stake. The print will be issued by a single printmaker, but then sold to many dealers, who will price them for resale as they see fit. Many of the print dealers will have no particular stake in the artist's reputation, and print dealers are not choosy about selecting buyers. Print buyers also tend to be less wealthy and less influential in the art world than buyers of paintings, contribute less to the artist's reputation, and therefore are charged the market-clearing price. Print buyers produce general fandom among a wide audience, but they provide less exclusive reputational capital to the artist. Discussing other fields, Taylor (1996, p. 4) gives a variety of examples of how an artist or writer acquired a successful posthumous reputation through the efforts of a spouse or a friend, often through the mechanism of shared reputational capital. On the collective nature of reputational production, see also Becker (1982), Mulkay and Chaplin (1982), Tompkins (1984), Kapsis (1989), and Taylor (1996, especially pp. 4–5).

24. In more technical economic language, promotion for a star is determined by the profits available from an increase in demand, rather than by the change in social value produced, consumer surplus plus producer surplus. Profits and social value are not the same thing, and the profits from producing a good or service do not accurately measure its value to society. Rather the profits measure how much of the value can be captured by producers. The difference between profits and social value arises because consumers/fans do not typically buy advertisements in a separate market, but rather receive ads for free from suppliers. In most cases the transactions costs of buying advertisements would be very high; we cannot easily imagine mechanisms for charging fans for billboards, for public displays, or for individual advertisements on television. Fans therefore cannot bid for the most valuable pieces of advertising information. The supply of ads

ends up being driven by supplier profits, rather than by consumer preferences and net social benefit.

25. Similarly, unauthorized copies and reproductions limit the incentive for payola. Although unauthorized cassette copies of recordings boost the fame of the creator by spreading the product, they decrease the returns to payola, and decrease the returns to fame promotion. To the extent that praise for sale refines and improves critical opinion, copyright should be enforced strictly. Copyright enforcement will maintain the potential for profit and strengthen the incentive for commercial promotion. But if critical opinion is more effective or more "correct" in the absence of promotion, copyright enforcement should be correspondingly weaker. Pirated editions limit the incentive for the original performer to invest in product promotion.

26. Some of the effects of payola on the demand for music, however, may be for *future* recordings, which cannot necessarily be produced at decreasing costs.

27. Audiences, of course, are aware of this tendency to some degree, and adjust their expectations accordingly. For this reason, rational audiences may prefer to listen to very well-established critics. Audiences know that these critics do not rely on favors for further advancement, and thus they are more likely to make negative comments when appropriate.

28. See Posner (1990, p. 61).

29. On Orwell, see Rodden (1984); on the French Revolution, see Furet (1981, passim, especially p. 10). Note that the strategy of ambiguity does not succeed in all contexts. Ambiguous production yields the highest potential returns when critics behave entrepreneurially, rather than reactively or conservatively. An enterprising critic may succeed in being the first to present a new interpretation of Keynes or Orwell, for instance, perhaps in the form of a critical study or monograph, thus enhancing the fame of the book's subject. But conservative critics are likely to more cautious when faced with works rich in ambiguity, withholding praise or skimping coverage, thus not augmenting the renown of the works' creators, for reasons discussed in Chapter 4. Performers and creators know that it is harder to induce

conservatively inclined critics to behave entrepreneurially, and they respond by making their performances and works clearer, less deep, and less ambiguous. A novelist of ideas usually benefits more from being ambiguous than an economist submitting an article to a professional journal.

30. As Klein (1997) points out, third-party certifiers, such as critics and disc jockeys, have incentives to issue reliable recommendations. Fans also may know that if a critic takes bribes, that critic has a strong incentive to seek out the best performers looking to break into the market. The disc jockeys who took payola in the 1950s went to great lengths to discover new musical stars (Cowen 1998, chap. 4), knowing that they could profit from praising such performers.

31. See Cairncross (1997, p. 125), Tagliabue (1997), and Neuborne (1998).

32. See Sudjic (1989, pp. 11, 52–53) and Phillips (1997). On the twenty percent estimate, see Agrawal and Kamakura (1995, p. 56). On Clark, see Leibovich (1999).

33. Nelson (1974) provides the classic treatment of advertising and signaling. For marketing theories of endorsements and related approaches, see Agrawal and Kamakura (1995), Ohanian (1990), and McCracken (1989).

3 THE NEW HEROES AND ROLE MODELS

1. See Churchill's essay "Mass Effects in Modern Life" (1990 [1932], p. 191). Other commentators who make similar criticisms include Schlesinger (1961), Schickel (1985), Roche (1987), Mitroff and Bennis (1989), James (1993), Salisbury (1993), and Gamson (1994).

2. See Plutarch (n.d., p. 293). See also the collection of Plutarch's essays (1993). This volume also contains his "Rules for Politicians," which offers other relevant observations about fame-seeking; see pp. 173–175.

3. See Averill (1950).

4. For the list of figures most admired, see Fowles (1992, p. 165). For the Elvis stamp, see Rodman (1996, pp. 90–91).

5. See *Scott Specialized Catalogue of United States Stamps* (1994).

6. On biographies, see Lowenthal (1956, 1961, chap. 4). Lowenthal defines the "serious" arts as "literature, fine arts, music, dance, and theater".

7. See Friedman (1990, p. 119), Meyrowitz (1985, p. 168), Ginsberg (1990, p. 25), and Cappella and Jamieson (1997, p. 18). On Roosevelt, see Collins (1998, p. 146).

8. Meyrowitz (1985) stresses how scrutiny gives rise to disillusionment with politics.

9. Schwartz (1987, pp. 194–199).

10. On how the British monarchy has changed with the media, see Spoto (1995).

11. On related points, see Ehrenhalt (1991) and Sutter (1998).

12. On the loss of shame in contemporary American society, see Twitchell (1997).

13. See Hirschman (1970). More generally, the greater potency of approbation in the large—fame—tends to imply lesser importance for approbation in the small. In the United States, with its many national heroes, fame is relatively easy to achieve. The sources of social publicity are numerous and diverse and the large size of the market supports renown for many performers. At the same time, most Americans, compared to inhabitants of other countries, do not care greatly what their neighbors think of them. The influence of local praise and shame has weakened over time, as traditional norms have been preempted by modern commercial society. The situation is different in lesser developed countries, such as Albania. These countries do not have the technology or resources to disseminate information about a large number of achievers and celebrities. Social publicity is produced less efficiently, there are fewer ways of earning fame, and the size of the market is much smaller. Yet approbation in the Albanian village is more powerful than in the United States. If Albania ever becomes a modernized capitalist democracy, achieving fame will become easier and the approbational influence of the village will decline, as has happened throughout Western Europe.

14. Morgan and Reynolds (1997) discuss in detail the inability of contemporary politicians to get away with public gaffes and errors.

15. These differences stem from underlying differences in how reciprocal exchange operates in politics and in the market for goods. Democratic political fame is produced concurrently with voting, whereas the fame of entertainers is produced concurrently with purchase of the product. The special role of voting in politics gives a special place to the winner, while neutralizing the role of the loser and those who never ran for office in the first place.

16. On the economics of brand names, see Barzel (1982) and also Gambetta (1994).

17. Shrum (1996) suggests that critics adopt systematically tougher standards for high culture than for popular culture, and systematically apply higher standards to performers with higher aspirations. Again, these evolved practices increase the efficiency of the reciprocal exchange of praise for performance. Shrum (1996, chap. 7, pp. 150–157) found that the status of the relevant genre as high culture or low culture accounted for the positive biases of some reviews and the negative bias in others; performers in the most "popular" genres were most likely to garner favorable reviews. Shrum also found (p. 153) that critics' informal reviews of the more popular shows did not reflect higher standards, but that when translating their opinions into print, the critics applied a looser standard.

18. Cervantes also treated fame in *Journey to Parnassus* (1883 [1614]). On related themes, see the modern writings of Fukuyama (1992). On "doux commerce," see Hirschman (1977).

19. On Greek mythology, see Mikalson (1991, pp. 31, 36). See Hobbes (1990, chap. 10, p. 67) and paragraph 116, p. 181 in Locke (1989 [1693]). For Adam Smith on martial virtue, see book 5, chap. 1 of *Wealth of Nations*. For him, martial virtue declines through the division of labor, not the multiplication of fame; see Smith (1937 [1776], p. 659).

20. See Saint Augustine (1950, p. 172). On Milton, see Freeman (1980). A related tradition in Chinese thought provides a skeptical attitude as well: "The great man is a public misfortune," claims one Chinese proverb (Lubin 1968, p. 117).

21. On female heroines in Greek thought, see Larson (1995) and Lyons (1997).

22. On the general theme, see Paulson (1989, chap. 4) and Barker-Banfield (1992, chap. 3). The quotations are from Rousseau (1968 [1758], pp. 71, 117).

23. See Rawson (1969, p. 1).

24. Carlyle (1993 [1840], p. 169). On the views of Carlyle, see Fowles (1992, p. 11).

25. See Fowles (1992, pp. 261–262) and Russell (1993, p. 31).

26. On television and violence, see Hamilton (1998). As for relative quantities, in television programming, for example, the mean ratings of violent programs actually have been falling over time. Paik and Comstock (1994) survey the literature on the effects of simulations on actual violent behavior.

27. See Fukuyama (1992, p. 316) and Becker (1994, pp. 17–18, 24–25).

4 THE TEST OF TIME

1. Schopenhauer (1936, p. 96).

2. On Melville and Wilde, see the remarks of Meyer (1998); on Agee and Evans, see Orvell (1995, p. 57).

3. On the evolution of the procedures for awarding Nobel Prizes, see Crawford (1984). On cooperation in long-lived institutions, see Cremer (1986). On collective reputational discipline in organizations, see Tirole (1996).

4. On the structure and organization of the baseball Hall of Fame, see James (1994, pp. 6, 36, 288–290, chap. 23). On the nonprofit status of Halls of Fame in general, see, for instance, Springwood (1996, p. 42). On trust motives and nonprofits, see Hansemann (1980, 1987). For-profit motives do influence the baseball Hall of Fame, but in largely beneficial fashion. Clark Estates, the charitable foundation that operates and controls the Hall, also controls the Adirondack Corporation as well as several other for-profit corporations in the Cooperstown area, including hotels and real estate (James 1994, pp. 288–289). Cooperstown is a relatively small town, and the profits of these corporations depend largely upon the ability of the Hall of Fame to attract a substantial tourist trade. If the Hall lost its status and reputation, the

tourist traffic would dry up, and the for-profit corporations of Clark Estates would suffer. In this case profit motives support the prestige of the Hall indirectly, but the selection procedures remain insulated from for-profit pressures.

5. See James (1994, pp. 246–248, 257–258, chap. 19). There were, however, times when the baseball Hall lowered its standards. Induction into the Hall can be granted *either* by the vote of sportswriters *or* by the Veterans Committee, composed of players. The dual voting structure created looser standards than the unitary voting system alone and Hall standards declined at times. Sometimes members of the Veterans Committee voted for the induction of players who were their friends without sufficient regard for the quality of their performance. In 1978, the Hall responded by limiting the power of the Veterans Committee and reinforcing high standards (James 1994, pp. 48, 299–300, passim). On the nonprofit status of most Halls of Fame, see Danilov (1997, p. 2).

6. On the Booker Prize, see Todd (1996, pp. 61–62).

7. For a discussion of the great attention paid to Michelin rankings and the lesser status of other food critics, including Gault-Milleau, see Echikson (1995).

8. "Public Television: The Taxpayer's Wagner" (1992, p. 41). Contrary to what some think, public television is funded primarily by the private sector; government grants account for only 17 percent of the public television budget.

9. Taylor (1996, p. 244) also argues that contemporary fame is fragile and evanescent.

10. Soderberg, Washington, and Press (1977, p. xii).

11. See Cowen (1998).

12. For the list of the ten most quoted writers, see Krantz (1997, p. 64).

13. These monopolies owe their existence partly to reputational efficiencies. Fans often find a dominant or monopoly critic easier to observe and monitor. Readers and fans consult the Michelin guides, in part, because they can evaluate a long-established, highly influential critic more easily than a less famous one. The ratings of the Michelin guides have a dramatic impact on the fortunes of restaurants and the

demand for their services, and thus are scrutinized with fervor. The editors know that their mistakes will be found and therefore they take great care to avoid mistakes. The Michelin guides are read because they have high standards, but the causality runs the other way as well; Michelin guides have high and coherent standards because they are read.

14. On Owen, see James (1988, pp. 33–35).

15. On van Gogh, see Rosenfeld (1998, p. A1).

16. On the rising fame of the Bloomsbury group, see Marler (1997).

17. Bristol (1996) shows how the fame of Shakespeare has been enhanced by marketable commodities, such as film adaptations and Shakespeare T-shirts.

18. For other examples of fame related to premature death, see Taylor (1996, p. 73).

19. Degrees of favoritism differ across genres. In some fields, such as the American cinema, the gap between critical expertise and popular taste is relatively small. Most moviegoers believe that their own evaluations are no worse than those of the critics (English 1979, pp. 111, 117). The endorsements of movie critics matter less for careers in films than in other endeavors, and critics have relatively few opportunities for favoritism. In the art world, by contrast, the critic typically has a much keener eye than the casual viewer. Endorsements are more important and favoritism will increase accordingly. Critical favoritism also is stronger in the more arcane genres and in complex high culture than in popular culture. Female authors have had an especially large presence and high status in genre writing for the mass market, such as romances and detective stories.Females, minorities, and other victims of discrimination also encounter more critical success in the popular music market than in the realm of contemporary classical composition. Popular culture, high monetary stakes, weak roles for critics, and relatively equal opportunity tend to be found together.

Payola is, in part, a market response to the discriminatory powers of critics. Performers pay the critic for endorsements, rather than allowing critics to choose their personal favorites. In effect, payola makes the critic pay a price for discriminating; critics forgo payola income when they recommend their nephews. Payola therefore gives individuals a chance to buy their way into markets that they otherwise could not crack. Not surprisingly, record industry payola has been used most heavily by outsiders and minorities, such as blacks, who had to battle discrimination (Cowen 1998, chap, 4).

20. On the Matthew effect, see Merton (1973). On the citations literature, see Cronin (1984) and Lang and Lang (1990, p. 342).

21. The audience for scientific research also encourages centralized credit. The costs of processing information make it easier for observers to associate a single dominant name with a given scientific contribution, thereby lowering their costs of attribution and search. The audience demand for diversified credit among scientists is relatively weak. Music fans want to enjoy many stars, but in science the audience cares primarily about the contribution, not the fair allocation of the credit for the contribution.

22. Schopenhauer (1960 [1851], pp. 82–83).

23. Critics also protect their favorite performers from the critical barbs of others, or try to create Matthew effects deliberately. Many speakers trumpet their preferences loudly in advance to create a snowballing of support. If a candidate for an academic job who was initially supported by only a few faculty members appears certain to be hired, other faculty members will throw their support behind that candidate because they want to be on the winning side.

24. Rodden (1989, p. 58).

25. On *Source,* see George (1998, p. 71).

26. See Montaigne (1967, p. 267), in his essay "Of Honorary Awards." Schopenhauer (1936, p. 52) regards national pride as the cheapest and basest sort of pride because it is shared by so many people.

27. On medals, see Shenon (1996, p. 5), Klapp (1991, pp. 125–131). On the history of medals in the United Kingdom, see Wilson and McEwen (1939).

28. See Holmes (1986, pp. 356–357), Klapp (1991, p. 128), and Shenon (1996, p. 5).

29. See Macken (1910), Kemp (1948), Woodward (1990), Bohlen (1997), and Haller (1997) on the history of canonization procedures.

30. Medal inflation also may signal that the U.S. government is optimistic about the future of warfare. The debasement of military fame would be less rapid if governments expected to face critical wars in the near future. Military fame debasement started after World War II, when America's security was extremely high and a nuclear deterrent was in place. Countries resort to medal inflation either when the end of their government is near or when high levels of security allow them to use up some of their reputational capital without great fear of negative repercussions in the future. America falls into the latter category.

31. See Klapp (1991, p. 11). Dale Carnegie, in his bestseller *How to Win Friends and Influence People*, wrote: "Rule 2, Smile." Many people bought Carnegie's book and smiled. Through the influence of Carnegie and others, smiles began to mean less. A smile was no longer a special mark of approval; it had become an expected response. People who did not smile eventually were perceived as gruff, unfriendly, and perhaps even hostile. Similar erosions of meaning have brought on the growing acceptability of obscenity. The placement of the word "fuck" in an artwork is no longer a cause for great consternation, at least if no government funding is involved. Artists are now relatively free to use obscenities but, not accidentally, they also find it increasingly difficult to achieve the desired shock effect. Similarly, "giving the finger" no longer carries the insult value that it once did. Of course, sometimes we welcome the debasement of language, as when terms of opprobrium formerly used to characterize minorities lose their sting. Ethnic slurs arguably have less force today than they did forty years ago, in part because American public discourse has diminished the shock value of almost any epithet.

I drew upon Klapp (1991, p. 138) for the Carnegie example. On the toughening of talk over time, see Plotnik (1996, chap. 9); on exaggeration in science, see Brown (1974).

32. Landes and Posner (1987, p. 271) discuss trademarks, such as "Kleenex" and "Xerox," that have now become generic designations.

33. For a survey and critique of the "language critics," largely on the basis of their elitism, see Daniels (1983). On whether languages

progress or decay, from a linguist's point of view, see Aitchison (1991). For a critical analysis of the development of public discourse, see Habermas (1989).

5 THE PROLIFERATION OF FAME

1. See Rosen (1981). The quotation is from Frank and Cook (1995, p. 61). Frank and Cook (1995, pp. 7, 43) trace the winner-take-all argument back to Alfred Marshall.

2. Frank and Cook make normative arguments that the superstars phenomenon is undesirable. The analysis of Rosen (1981) implies that the superstars effect is welfare-improving (all consumers receive the best performer) even if it leads to income inequality.

3. The figures are taken from Whitburn (1997). On the diversity of the 1990s, see Burnett (1996, p. 115).

4. The data are from Whitburn (1997). To construct the index, I took the top 100 albums of the period 1955–1996, as defined by weeks spent at the number-one position on the *Billboard* charts, and added up the number of weeks that each album spent at number one for each decade; and then I divided by the number of years in the decade. The division by number of years is necessary because we do not have full data for either the 1950s or the 1990s.

5. The data are from Whitburn (1997).

6. See Burnett (1990, p. 132).

7. For the statistic on the decline of the networks' audiences, see Medved (1992, p. 5). On *Seinfeld,* see Rich (1998, p. 56).

8. On Frank and the cinema, see Shea (1998, p. A14); see also Frank and Cook (1995, pp. 72–77).

9. The data on movie grosses are taken from the web site <www.vex.net/~odin/Gross/>.

10. The source is *The Bowker Annual Library and Book Trade Alamanac, 1974–1998.* The figures include both fiction and nonfiction.

11. On the publishing history of Foxe's book, see Haller (1963, pp. 13–14). On the history of Bunyan's book, see Starker (1989, p. 54) and Furlong (1975, passim and p. 180). For figures on book sales, see

Cowen (1998, chap. 2, drawn from the *Statistical Abstract of the United States*).

12. See Cowen and Normann (1999). Frank and Cook (1995, pp. 65–66) argue that rewards have become increasingly centralized, but their data source (an unpublished honors thesis at Cornell by Chadwick Meyer) considers only the earlier years of the sample, whereas Cowen and Normann bring the sample up to the present. The latter years change the result fundamentally, since rewards have lately become more decentralized. Frank and Cook also do not consider the issue of correlation with Nielsen ratings, which Cowen and Normann take as a proxy for reproducibility.

13. See Temkin (1993) on this theme.

14. On the complementarity of fame in another realm, that of architecture, see the remarks of Williamson (1990, p. 225).

15. See Creamer (1992, p. 227) and James (1988, p. 422).

16. See Gould (1966).

17. Tenner (1996, pp. 238–239).

18. Whether the convergence of quality argument applies to politics requires partisan judgments about the meaning of "quality," and thus judgments about the proper role of government. But if we define the quality of politicians in terms of their own ends only, rather than in terms of an external standard for "best policy," convergence of quality again appears to hold. Today's fifth best presidential candidate is probably closer in political talent to the best than was the case a hundred years ago. The pool of potential candidates is larger and they have more handlers and get more expert advice than earlier candidates.

19. On minor league baseball, see James (1988, pp. 80–83). See also James's remarks (1994, chap. 18) on the application of Gould's quality convergence thesis to baseball. Thorn and Palmer (1984, chaps. 6 and 7) provide statistical evidence that the overall quality of baseball has improved over time.

20. See Hirsch (1973). On zero-sum fame and status, see also McAdams (1992), Frank (1984), Frank and Cook (1995), and Schor (1996).

21. On British literary prizes, see Todd (1996, pp. 57, 95, passim).

22. On the history of the World Cup, see Lewis (1998).

23. See James (1988). See also Thorn and Palmer (1984), who develop a variety of complex statistics to measure baseball performance over time. On gymnastics, see Guttmann (1978, pp. 50–51).

24. Of course, statistics do not internalize all potential gains from trade between fans and stars. Numbers do not themselves direct strategic behavior or resolve the problem of underprovision of fandom. Statistics must be supported by some independent set of coordinating institutions, such as critics or fan conventions, that focus on numerical performance.

25. Marler (1997, p. 191).

26. On multidimensionality and fame, see Taylor (1996, p. 64).

27. On the Booker Prize, see Todd (1996, p. 74).

28. See Plutarch (n.d., pp. 131, 293).

29. On the Barnard Medal, see Cole and Cole (1981, p. 56); on the Hall of Fame, see Smith (1982, pp. 62–64).

30. On the Nobel Prizes, see Crawford (1984, chap. 7); on the Pulitzer Prizes, see Rothmyer (1991, pp. 3–4).

31. In this paragraph I draw heavily on Cooley (1927). He writes, for instance, "the Hebrew nation and history, as we have it in the Bible . . . unites patriarchs, kings, prophets, apostles and minor characters in one vast symbol" (p. 121).

32. The definitions and weights change over time, and may well have changed by the time this book appears; my source is Early (1989, p. 115).

33. On the Indiana debate, see Bradsher (1996) and Gildea (1997). In Indiana high school basketball draws large crowds and is extremely popular. Fifteen of the country's sixteen largest high school gyms are in Indiana, with the largest seating 9,314 spectators.

34. On the Athletics versus the Yankees, see the comments of Barra (1998).

35. The Goethe quotation is from Bate (1970, p. 96). On Japanese archery, see Tenner (1996, pp. 235, 322). On Hume, see Hume (1985 [1777], pp. 135–137). For other proponents of this view, see Lowenthal (1985, chap. 3, especially p. 93).

36. Hazlitt (1948 [1814], pp. 607–609).

37. Fame-seekers are made worse off by the burden of the past, because they must try harder to win fame, and to reward new stars appropriately, we will have to take fame away from previous performers. Revisionist historians and critics, insofar as they disseminate negative or skeptical views of great achievers of the past and present, help wipe the fame slate clean and encourage future achievements. In effect, revisionism counters the burden of the past by making past achievement more fragile.

38. On Marcellinus, see the notes to Longinus' *On the Sublime* (1985, p. 81). On the eighteenth-century tradition, see Scheffer (1936).

6 THE DARK SIDE OF FAME

1. Among modern writers on celebrity, Fowles (1992) and Berlin (1996) devote the most attention to the burdens of fame. The Power quotation is taken from the unnumbered photo insert in Fowles (1992). On Green, see Green (1996, p. 242).

2. Lyall (1987) and Riding (1997).

3. On the history of wax museums, see Chapman (1992) and Riding (1997).

4. On some of these episodes, see Fowles (1992, pp. 133–136).

5. Hume (1985 [1777], p. 120).

6. Naive Art encompasses a wide gamut of styles, and has been prominent in such diverse places as the former Yugoslavia, Haiti, the African-American community, and Swiss insane asylums. For a recent and laudatory history of Naive Art and its discovery by art critics, see Maizels (1996).

7. On Pierce, see Livingston and Beardsley (1982, p. 121).

8. On these artists, and others, see Gitter and Rae Yelen (1995) and Maresca and Ricco (1993).

9. For some economic models where the quest for reputation induces conformity, see Scharfstein and Stein (1990) and Zwiebel (1995). On the benefits of amateur science, see Kealey (1996, pp. 86–88).

10. See Nagel (1995, p. 8).

11. See, for instance, Wise (1998), who discusses the decline of team play and traces it to the star system.

12. On related themes involving sex, see Shalit (1999).

13. Socrates, in the *Symposium* (1956, p. 375), claims that we will run all risks for fame, which serves as a kind of immortality. On risk-taking and tournaments, see Brenner (1987, 1990).

14. On these points, see "The Merged Book Market" (1998, p. 15).

15. On Japan, see Hechter and Kanazawa (1993). Ehrenhalt (1996) notes a pervasive lack of individual privacy in the strong communities he examines in the United States.

16. See Kuran (1995) and Scharfstein and Stein (1990).

17. See Klein and Leffler (1981) and Klein (1997) on the market-oriented views.

18. On superconductivity, see Hagen (1980).

19. On Byrd, see Wilford (1996) and Bryce (1997). On the quest for medals, Lieutenant-Colonel Peter Halford-Thompson remarked, "Hunting of decorations is a menace. A fellow officer was determined to get a bar to his MC. He became a very dangerous bore and caused many unnecessary casualties before he himself was killed. The very brave . . . are often quiet people doing their job superlatively well under fire" (Holmes 1986, p. 358).

20. See Brown (1968) and Baumeister (1997).

21. On compliance professionals and the use of approbational incentives in sales, see Cialdini (1984, chap. 5).

22. See Hašek (1930, pp. 29–30) and Mandeville (1988 [1735], vol. 1, p. 75). Evidence from experimental psychology indicates that individuals sometimes behave more vindictively when others are watching. They do not mind taking a private loss, but they feel disgraced by a public loss, and often will retaliate, even when retaliation brings no material benefit (Brown 1968; Baumeister 1997, pp. 133–1334). In addition, crowds and spectators sometimes encourage homicide. Despite strong practical reasons for wanting to avoid witnesses, many murderers act only in a crowd; one extensive study of California homicides found that an audience was present in more than half the cases (Luckenbill 1977; Baumeister 1997, p. 156).

23. The quotation is from Semple (1993, p. 140). Bentham took the use of the polygonal form to facilitate observation from the military practices of Tsarist Russia (1969, p. 196). And although the British government never erected prisons on the Panopticon plan, one government later in this century did: Gerardo Machado's Cuban dictatorship in 1932 (Ryle 1996). Interestingly, Bentham's earlier and more general theory of the passions mentioned fame and reputation but did not place critical weight on those motivations. His classic *Introduction to the Principles of Morals and Legislation* cites love of reputation but devotes less than a page of discussion to the topic. John Stuart Mill, in his famous essay on Bentham, even chides Bentham for placing so little weight on the motivations of pride, fame, and honor. See Bentham (1982 [1780], pp. 105–106, 135). Also see Bentham's "Psychology of Economic Man" (1954), where the emphasis on approbation is even weaker. For Mill on Bentham, see Mill (1950 [1838], p. 67)]. I am indebted to David Levy for valuable discussions about Bentham's work, especially the Auto-Icon plan.

24. For the relevant passages, see Bentham (1969, p. 199, passim), Semple (1993, p. 288), Semple (1993, p. 143), and Semple (1993, p. 288). Semple (1993, pp. 3–5) surveys other views that identify the Panopticon as Bentham's intended model for broader society. See also Ignatieff (1978) on this point.

25. See also the notes of Mack in Bentham (1969, pp. 189–193).

26. Bentham (1832, p. 3).

27. Bentham (1832, p. 3.

28. Bentham (1832, pp. 3-6).

29. Bentham (1832, p. 7).

30. Spoto (1993, p. 667).

31. For this interpretation of fame in Homer, see Griffin (1980, chap. 3). For the Achilles quotation, see Homer's *Odyssey*, (1963, p. 201, book 11, line 469). The proverb is taken from the opening section of Berlin (1996), no page number.

32. For the quotation, see *Henry VI, Part I*, Act I, scene 1, line 6.

33. See Fowles, (1992, pp. 236–238). Wills and Cooper (1988) document the stress faced by popular musicians, including evidence

acquired through surveys and questionnaires; see, for instance, p. 54. On the stresses of exercising power, see Kayden (1990). Mitroff and Bennis (1989, pp. 116–117) provide a ledger of the psychological costs of fame. Valhouli (1998) provides evidence on rock star deaths.

34. For these quotations, see Berlin (1996, pp. 3, 29, 33).

35. See Pascal (1995 [1670], pp. 25-26).

36. Smith (1981 [1759], pp. 124-125).

37. See Kojève (1969, p. 46).

38. See Warhol (1975. p. 84).

39. The Valentino quotation is from Goodman (1997). On Davis, see McCann (1996, p. 236).

40. See Westie (1973).

41. See Boethius (1963 [523?], pp. 56–58).

42. *Divine Comedy* (1993, pp. 245-246).

43. See Boccaccio's *Amorosa Visione* (1986, p. 123), and Petrarch's *Triumphs* (1962), especially the section "The Triumph of Time." The quotation is from p. 99. The metaphor of fame as a second death is borrowed from Boethius (1963 [523?], p. 58). For a pagan presentation of the vainglory of fame-seeking, see Persius' Satire 10 (1961, p. 205). For a later view, consistent with the Stoic account, see Schopenhauer (1936, pp. 46–47, passim).

44. *Henry IV, Part I* (1994, p. 195, Act 5, scene 2, lines 131–142).

45. See Saint Augustine (1950, p. 164), Montaigne's essay "Of Glory," (1967, book 2, essay 16), and Cicero's "Pro Archia Poeta"(1979, p. 35). On Tacitus, see Schopenhauer (1936, p. 50).

46. On fame as an addiction, see Berlin (1996, pp.xv, 284). The Smith quotation is from Smith (1981 [1759], p. 57). For a psychological study of how the receipt of fame diminishes concern about other areas of life, and alienates the self, see Adler and Adler (1989). Neapolitan (1988) argues that addiction to praise incentives may even diminish the desire to perform the praised task. On the psychosociology of the famous, see also Goertzel, Goertzel, and Goertzel (1978). George McKenzie (in Vickers 1986, p. 20 [1666, p. 12]) also described the ambition for recognition as an addiction that feeds upon itself. On the economics of self-constraint more generally, see, for instance, Elster

(1979), Schelling (1984), Ainslie (1992), and Cowen (1991), among others.

47. Hauser (1991, p. 399).

48. Baden-Guest (1996, p. 197).

49. See Frank (1989). This phenomenon has plausible evolutionary microfoundations. If the happiness of an individual adjusts to current circumstances, that individual will strive for more no matter how much he or she has already achieved. Such individuals may have better chances of surviving and reproducing than individuals who become content with a high level of absolute achievement. The evolution of such preferences would represent a victory of our genes over our personal well-being.

50. In economic language, the renowned, by receiving an "efficiency wage" in the form of their recognition, have little opportunity to shirk.

51. Spinoza (1951, p. 4).

52. See Epictetus' *Discourses* (1940, especially pp. 273, 336, 387).

53. See Addison (1987 [1711], p. 491). The McKenzie quotation is from Vickers (1986, p. 6), but was originally written in 1666.

7 LESSONS FOR THE FUTURE

1. Ashley (1947 [1596?], p. 30).

2. Robert H. Frank (1999), for instance, has suggested a progressive consumption tax to check the winner-take-all society, among other market failures.

3. On status motives for charity, see Ostrower (1995). Glazer and Konrad (1996) demonstrate the importance of meeting a threshold standard for recognition.

4. In expressing his desire to constrain fame-seeking, Hobbes was addressing a problem raised by Christianity, but he realized that religion had lost its force; belief alone did not curb the rapacious appetites of fame-seekers. Not only was Hobbes an atheist, but he thought that the potential torments of Hell, in the eyes of believers, were not strong enough to ensure moral behavior on earth. Hobbes therefore sought to

replace religious incentives with the absolute force of the sovereign, thus giving rise to his concept of Leviathan. For Hobbes's views on why religious incentives do not ensure moral behavior, see chap. 38 of *Leviathan*. Hobbes (1991 [1651], chap. 38, p. 313) argues that Scripture does not support the view that Hell involves infinite pain.

5. Hobbes (1991 [1651], p. 128).

References

Adair, Douglass. 1974. "Fame and the Founding Fathers." In *Fame and the Founding Fathers: Essays by Douglass Adair,* ed. Trevor Colburn, pp. 3–26. New York: W. W. Norton.

Adams, John. 1851 [1790]. *Discourses on Davila.* In *The Works of John Adams,* vol. 6, pp. 226–403. Boston: Charles C. Little and James Brown.

Addison, Joseph. 1987. *The Spectator.* Edited with an introduction by Donald F. Bond. Oxford: Clarendon Press.

Adler, Moshe. 1985. "Stardom and Talent." *American Economic Review,* 1985, 75: 208–212.

Adler, Patricia A., and Peter Adler. 1989. "The Gloried Self: The Aggrandizement and Construction of Self." *Social Psychology Quarterly,* 52 (4): 299–310.

Agrawal, Jagdish, and Wagner A. Kamakura. 1995. "The Economic Worth of Celebrity Endorsers: An Event Study Analysis." *Journal of Marketing,* 59: 56–62.

Ainslee, George. 1992. *Picoeconomics.* Cambridge: Cambridge University Press.

Aitchison, Jean. 1991. *Language Change: Progress or Decay?* Cambridge: Cambridge University Press.

Akerlof, George A. 1984. *An Economic Theorist's Book of Tales: Essays That Entertain the Consequences of New Assumptions in Economic Theory.* Cambridge: Cambridge University Press.

Alexander, David. 1994. *Star Trek Creator: The Authorized Biography of Gene Roddenberry.* New York: Penguin.

Alighieri, Dante. 1993. *The Divine Comedy,* trans. C. H. Sisson. Oxford: Oxford University Press.

Ashley, Robert. 1947 [1596?]. *Of Honour.* Edited by Virgil B. Heltzel. San Marino, Calif.: Huntington Library.

Augustine, Saint. 1950. *The City of God.* New York: Modern Library.

Ault, Wayne. 1981. *Show Business and Politics: The Influence of Television, Entertainment Celebrities, and Motion Pictures on American Public Opinion and Political Behavior.* Ann Arbor, Mich.: University Microfilms.

Averill, Lawrence A. 1950. "The Impact of a Changing Culture upon Pubescent Ideals." *School and Society,* July 22, pp. 49–52.

Bacon-Smith, Camille. 1992. *Enterprising Women: Television Fandom and the Creation of Popular Myth.* Philadelphia: University of Pennsylvania Press.

Baden-Guest, Anthony. 1996. *True Colors: The Real Life of the Art World.* New York: Atlantic Monthly Press.

Bailie, Gil. 1995. *Violence Unveiled: Humanity at the Crossroads.* New York: Crossroad.

Barker-Banfield, G. J. 1992. *The Culture of Sensibility: Sex and Society in Eighteenth-Century Britain.* Chicago: University of Chicago Press.

Barra, Allen. 1998. "Team." In the feature article "Overrated and Underrated." *Forbes American Heritage,* June, pp. 66–67.

Barrow, Joe Louis, Jr., and Barbara Munder. 1988. *Joe Louis: Fifty Years an American Hero.* New York: McGraw-Hill.

Barzel, Yoram. 1982. "Measurement Cost and the Organization of Markets." *Journal of Law and Economics,* 25: 27–46.

Bate, Walter Jackson. 1970. *The Burden of the Past and the English Poet.* Cambridge: Harvard University Press.

Baumeister, Roy F. 1997. *Evil: Inside Human Violence and Cruelty.* New York: W. H. Freeman.

Bayley, C. C. 1961. *War and Society in Renaissance Florence: The "De Militia" of Leonardo Bruni.* Toronto: University of Toronto Press.

Becker, Gary S. 1991. "A Note on Restaurant Pricing and Other Examples of Social Influence on Price." *Journal of Political Economy,* 99: 1109–1116.

———1992. "Habits, Addictions, and Traditions." *Kyklos,* 45: 327–345.

———1996. *Accounting for Tastes.* Cambridge: Harvard University Press.

Becker, Gary S. and Murphy, Kevin M. 1988. "A Theory of Rational Addiction." *Journal of Political Economy,* 96: 675–700.

Becker, Gary S., and Kevin M. Murphy. 1993. "A Simple Theory of Advertising as a Good or Bad." *Quarterly Journal of Economics,* 108: 941–964.

Becker, Howard S. 1982. *Art Worlds.* Berkeley: University of California Press.

Becker, Marvin B. 1994. *The Emergence of Civil Society in the Eighteenth Century: A Privileged Moment in the History of England, Scotland, and France.* Bloomington: Indiana University Press.

Bentham, Jeremy. 1832. "Auto-Icon; or, Farther Uses of the Dead to the Living. A Fragment." Unpublished.

———1954. "The Psychology of Economic Life." In *Jeremy Bentham's Economic Writings,* ed. W. Stark, pp. 421–450. London: George Allen & Unwin.

———1969. *Panopticon Papers.* In *A Bentham Reader,* ed. Mary Peter Mack, pp. 189–208. New York: Pegasus.

———1982 [1780]. *An Introduction to the Principles of Morals and Legislation.* London: Methuen.

Berlin, Joey. 1996. *Toxic Fame: Celebrities Speak on Stardom.* Detroit: Visible Ink.

Biagioli, Mario. 1993. *Galileo, Courtier: The Practice of Science in the Culture of Absolutism.* Chicago: University of Chicago Press.

Billacois, François. 1990. *The Duel: Its Rise and Fall in Early Modern France.* New Haven: Yale University Press.

Birkhead, Alice. 1913. *Heroes of Modern Europe.* New York: Thomas Y. Crowell Company.

Boccaccio, Giovanni. 1986. *Amorosa Visione*. Hanover, N.H.: University Press of New England.

Boethius, Anicius Manlius Severinus. 1963 [526?]. *The Consolation of Philosophy*. Carbondale: Southern Illinois University Press.

Bogart, Leo. 1995. *Commercial Culture: The Media System and the Public Interest*. New York: Oxford University Press.

Bohlen, Celestine. 1997. "Not If But When: Naming a Saint Isn't So Simple." *New York Times* (Washington ed.), Sept. 14, sect. 4, pp. 1, 4–6.

Boitani, Piero. 1984. *Chaucer and the Imaginary World of Fame*. Totowa, N.J.: Barnes & Noble.

Boorstin, Daniel J. 1987. *The Image: A Guide to Pseudo-Events in America*. New York: Atheneum.

Booth, John E. 1991. *The Critic, Power, and the Performing Arts*. New York: Columbia University Press.

Botting, Kate, and Douglas Botting. 1995. *Sex Appeal: The Art and Science of Sexual Attraction*. New York: St. Martin's Press.

Bourdieu, Pierre. 1984. *Distinction: A Social Critique of the Judgment of Taste*. Cambridge: Harvard University Press.

———1993. *The Field of Cultural Production: Essays on Art and Literature*. New York: Columbia University Press.

Bowker Annual Library and Book Trade Almanac, 1974–1998, The. New Providence, N.J.: R. R. Bowker.

Boyd, Malcolm. 1958. *Christ and Celebrity Gods: The Church in Mass Culture*. Greenwich, Conn.: Seabury Press.

Boyle, James. 1996. *Shamans, Software, and Spleens: Law and the Construction of the Information Society*. Cambridge: Harvard University Press.

Bradsher, Keith. 1996. "Ending the Dream of Giant-Killing: No Longer Will Small Battle Big for Indiana's Basketball Title." *New York Times,* May 9, p. A22.

Braudy, Leo. 1986. *The Frenzy of Renown: Fame and Its History*. New York: Oxford University Press.

Brennan, Geoffrey, and Philip Pettit. 1993. "Hands Invisible and Intangible." *Synthese*, 24: 191–225.

Brenner, Reuven. 1987. *Rivalry: In Business, Science, and among Nations.* Cambridge: Cambridge University Press.

———1990. *Gambling and Speculation: A Theory, a History, and a Future of Some Human Decisions.* New York: Cambridge University Press.

Bristol, Michael D. 1996. *Big-Time Shakespeare.* New York: Routledge.

Brown, Bert R. 1968. "The Effects of Need to Maintain Face on Interpersonal Bargaining." *Journal of Experimental Social Psychology,* 4: 107–122.

Brown, W. Bahngrell. 1974. "Language, Semantics, Hyperbole, Evolution, and the Literature of Science." *The Southern Quarterly,* 12: 287–294.

Brown, Rich. 1994. "Post-Sputnik Fandom (1957–1990)." In *Science Fiction Fandom,* ed. Joe Sanders, pp. 75–102. Westport, Conn.: Greenwood Press.

Bruce, Dickson D., Jr. 1979. *Violence and Culture in the Antebellum South.* Austin: University of Texas Press.

Bryce, Robert M. 1997. *Cook and Peary: A Polar Controversy Resolved.* Mechanicsburg, Penn.: Stackpole Books.

Burek, Deborah M., and Martin Connors, with Christa Brelin. 1992. *Organized Obsessions: 1001 Offbeat Associations, Fan Clubs, and Microsocieties You Can Join.* Detroit: Visible Ink Press.

Burnett, Robert. 1990. *Concentration and Diversity in the International Phonogram Industry.* Gothenburg: Gothenburg Studies in Journalism and Mass Communication.

———1996. *The Global Jukebox: The International Music Industry.* London: Routledge.

Burns, Thomas J., and Edward N. Coffman. 1976. *The Accounting Hall of Fame: Profiles of Thirty-Six Members.* Columbus: Ohio State University, College of Administrative Science.

Burton, Dee. *I Dream of Woody.* 1984. New York: William Morrow.

Calvert, Randall L. 1992. "Leadership and Its Basis in Problems of Social Coordination." *International Political Science Review,* 13: 7–24.

Cameron, Judy, and W. David Pierce. 1994. "Reinforcement, Reward, and Intrinsic Motivation: A Meta-Analysis." *Review of Educational Research,* 64: 363–423.

Cappella, Joseph N., and Kathleen Jamieson. 1997. *Spiral of Cynicism: The Press and the Public Good.* New York: Oxford University Press.

Carlyle, Thomas. 1993 [1840]. *On Heroes, Hero-Worship, and the Heroic in History.* Berkeley: University of California Press.

Carvajal, Doreen. 1997. "Book Jackets Are, by Definition, Shameless. Want Attention? Pan Your Own Author." *New York Times* (Washington ed.), Oct. 13, p. D7.

Cervantes Saavedra, Miguel de. 1883 [1614]. *Journey to Parnassus.* London: Kegan Paul, Trench and Co.

Chalmers, Alan D. 1995. *Jonathan Swift and the Burden of the Future.* Newark: University of Delaware Press.

Chapman, Pauline. 1992. *Madame Tussaud in England: Career Woman Extraordinary.* London: Quiller Press.

Churchill, Winston. 1990 [1932]. *Thoughts and Adventures.* New York: W. W. Norton.

Cialdini, Robert B. 1994. *Influence: How and Why People Agree to Things.* New York: William Morrow.

Cicero. 1979. "Pro Archia Poeta." In *Cicero in Twenty-Eight Volumes,* vol. 11, Loeb Classical Library. Cambridge: Harvard University Press.

Clawson, Calvin C. 1996. *Mathematical Mysteries: The Beauty and Magic of Numbers.* New York: Plenum Press.

Coase, Ronald H. 1979. "Payola in Radio and Television Broadcasting." *Journal of Law and Economics,* 22: 269–328.

Cole, Jonathan R., and Stephen Cole. 1973. *Social Stratification in Science.* Chicago: University of Chicago Press.

Coleman, James. 1990. *Foundations of Social Theory.* Cambridge: Harvard University Press.

Collins, Gail. 1998. *Scorpion Tongues: Gossip, Celebrity, and American Politics.* New York: William Morrow, 1998.

Condon, Dianne Russell. 1996. *Jackie's Treasures: The Fabled Objects from the Auction of the Century.* New York: Clarkson Publishers.

Cooley, Charles Horton. 1927. *Social Process.* New York: Charles Scribner's Sons.

Cornes, Richard, and Todd Sandler. 1996. *The Theory of Externalities, Public Goods, and Club Goods.* Cambridge: Cambridge University Press.

Cornwell, Sue, and Mike Kott. 1996. *Star Trek Collectibles,* 4th ed. New York: House of Collectibles.

Cottler, Joseph, and Haym Jaffee. 1931. *Heroes of Civilization.* Boston: Little, Brown.

Coulson. Robert. 1994. "Fandom as a Way of Life." In *Science Fiction Fandom,* ed. Joe Sanders, pp. 11—14. Westport, Conn.: Greenwood Press.

Cowen, Tyler. 1991. "Self-Liberation versus Self-Constraint," *Ethics,* 101: 360–373.

———1998. *In Praise of Commercial Culture.* Cambridge: Harvard University Press.

Cowen, Tyler, and Parker Normann. 1999. "Is Tennis a Superstars Market?" Unpublished ms., George Mason University.

Cowen, Tyler, and Daniel Sutter. 1997. "Politics and the Pursuit of Fame." *Public Choice,* 93: 19–35.

Crawford, Elisabeth. 1984. *The Beginnings of the Nobel Institution: The Science Prizes, 1901–1915.* Cambridge: Cambridge University Press.

Creamer, Robert W. 1992. *Babe: The Legend Comes to Life.* New York: Fireside.

Cremer, Jacques. 1986. "Cooperation in Ongoing Organizations." *Quarterly Journal of Economics,* 101: 33–49.

Crocker, Lester G. 1959. *An Age of Crisis: Man and World in Eighteenth Century French Thought.* Baltimore: The Johns Hopkins University Press.

Cronin, Blaise. 1984. *The Citation Process: The Role and Significance of Citations in Scientific Communication.* London: Taylor Graham.

Cronin, Thomas E., and Michael A. Genovese. 1998. *The Paradoxes of the American Presidency.* New York: Oxford University Press.

Daniels, Harvey A. 1983. *Famous Last Words: The American Language Crisis Reconsidered.* Carbondale: Southern Illinois University Press.

Danilov, Victor J. 1997. *Hall of Fame Museums: A Reference Guide.* Westport, Conn.: Greenwood Press.

Dawson, Doyne. 1996. *The Origins of Western Warfare: Militarism and Morality in the Ancient World.* Boulder: Westview Press.

deCordova, Richard. 1990. *Picture Personalities: The Emergence of the Star System in America.* Urbana: University of Illinois Press.

Delin, Catherine R., and Roy F. Baumeister. 1994. "Praise: More Than Just Social Reinforcement." *Journal for the Theory of Social Behaviour,* 24: 219–241.

Derrida, Jacques. 1981. *Dissemination.* Chicago: University of Chicago Press.

DeWitt, Howard A. 1985. *Chuck Berry: Rock 'N' Roll Music.* Ann Arbor, Mich.: Pierian Press.

"Diana (Let us Count the Ways)." 1998. In *Entertainment Weekly,* special year-end double issue, Dec. 26, 1997, Jan. 2, p. 100.

Diener, Ed. and Carol Diener. 1996. "Most People Are Happy." *Psychological Science,* 7: 181–185.

"Directory of Star Trek Organizations." 1997. Typescript. Distributed by Star Trek Welcommittee and Judy Segal.

Dodds, E. R. 1957. *The Greeks and the Irrational.* Boston: Beacon Press.

Donaldson, Scott. 1977. *By Force of Will: The Life and Art of Ernest Hemingway.* New York: Viking Press.

Donoghue, Frank. 1996. *The Fame Machine: Book Reviewing and Eighteenth-Century Literary Careers.* Stanford: Stanford University Press.

Douillet, Jacques. 1958. *What Is a Saint?* New York: Hawthorn Books.

Doyle, William. 1996. *Venality: The Sale of Offices in Eighteenth-Century France.* Oxford: Clarendon Press.

Dunbar, Robin. 1996. *Grooming, Gossip, and the Evolution of Language.* London: Faber and Faber.

Eagleton, Terry. 1987. *The Function of Criticism: From "The Spectator" to Post-Structuralism.* London: Verso Books.

Early, Gerald. 1989. *Tuxedo Junction: Essays on American Culture.* Hopewell, N.J.: Hopewell Press.

Echikson, William. 1995. *Burgundy Stars: A Year in The Life of a Great French Restaurant.* New York: Little, Brown.

Edwards, George C., III. 1990. *Presidential Approval: A Sourcebook.* Baltimore: The Johns Hopkins University Press.

Ehrenhalt, Alan. 1991. *The United States of Ambition: Politicians, Power and the Pursuit of Office.* New York: Times Books.

Ehrenreich, Barbara, Elizabeth Hess, and Gloria Jacobs. 1992. "Beatlemania: Girls Just Want to Have Fun." In *The Adoring Audience: Fan Culture and Popular Media,* ed. Lisa A. Lewis, pp. 84–106. London: Routledge.

Elias, Norbert. 1982. *The History of Manners.* New York: Pantheon Books.

Elster, Jon. 1979. *Ulysses and the Sirens.* Cambridge: Cambridge University Press.

Elton, Oliver. n.d. *Literary Fame: A Renaissance Study.* N.p.: privately printed.

Emerson, Ralph Waldo. n.d. *Representative Men.* Garden City, N.Y.: Dolphin Books.

English, John W. 1979. *Criticizing the Critics.* New York: Hastings House.

Epictetus. 1940. *Arrian's Discourses of Epictetus.* In *The Stoic and Epicurean Philosophers,* ed. Whitney Jennings Oates, pp. 221–457. New York: Modern Library.

Epstein, Joseph. 1980. *Ambition: The Secret Passion.* New York: E. P. Dutton.

Erasmus, Desiderius. 1971 [1536]. *Praise of Folly.* London: Penguin Books.

Ewen, Stuart. 1988. *All Consuming Images: The Politics of Style in Contemporary Culture.* New York: Basic Books.

Farnell, Lewis Richard. 1921. *Greek Hero Cults and Ideas of Immortality.* Oxford: Clarendon Press.

Fisher, Marc. 1997. "Jumpin' Jack Flashback: Graying Stones Fans Spend the Night Together and Watch as Thirty Years Go By." *Washington Post,* Oct. 23, pp. B1, B10.

Fishwick, Marshall W. 1954. *American Heroes: Myth and Reality.* Washington, D.C.: Public Affairs Press.

Fombrun, Charles, and Mark Shanley. 1990. "What's in a Name? Reputation Building and Corporate Strategy" *Academy of Management Journal,* 33: 233–258.

Fowles, Jib. 1992. *Starstruck: Celebrity Performers and the American Public.* Washington, D.C.: Smithsonian Institution Press.

Frank, Robert H. 1985. *Choosing the Right Pond: Human Behavior and the Quest for Status.* New York: Oxford University Press.

———1989. "Frames of Reference and the Quality of Life." *American Economic Review,* 79: 80–85.

———1999. *Luxury Fever.* New York: Free Press.

Frank, Robert H., and Philip J. Cook. 1995. *The Winner-Take-All Society: How More and More Americans Compete for Ever Fewer and Bigger Prizes, Encouraging Economic Waste, Income Inequality, and an Impoverished Cultural Life.* New York: Free Press.

Frazer, Sir James George. 1917. "The Magic Art and the Evolution of Kings." In Frazer's *The Golden Bough.* London: Macmillan.

Freeman, James A. 1980. *Milton and the Martial Muse: "Paradise Lost" and European Traditions of War.* Princeton: Princeton University Press.

Friar, Stephen, and John Ferguson. 1993. *Basic Heraldry.* New York: W. W. Norton.

Friedman, Lawrence M. 1990. *The Republic of Choice: Law, Authority, and Culture.* Cambridge: Harvard University Press.

Freud, Sigmund. 1961 [1927]. *The Future of an Illusion.* Garden City, N.Y.: Anchor Books.

Fuhrman, Candice Jacobson. 1989. *Publicity Stunt! Great Staged Events That Made the News.* San Francisco: Chronicle Books.

Fukuyama, Francis. 1992. *The End of History and the Last Man.* New York: Penguin.

Furet, François. 1981. *Interpreting the French Revolution.* Cambridge: Cambridge University Press.

Furlong, Monica. 1975. *Puritan's Progress.* New York: Coward, McCann, and Geoghegan.

Gambetta, Diego. 1994. "Inscrutable Markets." *Rationality and Society,* 6: 353–368.

Gambetta, Diego, ed. 1988. *Trust: Making and Breaking Cooperative Relations.* New York: Basil Blackwell.

Gamson, Joshua. 1994. *Claims to Fame: Celebrity in Contemporary America.* Berkeley: University of California Press.

George, Nelson. 1998. *Hip Hop America.* New York: Viking Penguin.

Gerhard, H. P. 1971. *The World of Icons.* New York: Harper & Row.

Gilbert, Robert E. 1992. *The Mortal Presidency: Illness and Anguish in the White House.* New York: Basic Books.

Gildea, William. 1997. *Where the Game Matters Most.* Boston: Little, Brown.

Girard, René. 1979. *Violence and the Sacred.* Baltimore: The Johns Hopkins University Press.

———1987. *Things Hidden since the Beginning of the World.* Stanford: Stanford University Press.

Gitter, Kurt, and Alice Rae Yelen. 1995. *Pictured in My Mind: Contemporary American Self-Taught Art.* Jackson: University Press of Mississippi.

Glazer, Amihai, and Kai A. Konrad. 1996. "A Signaling Explanation for Charity." *American Economic Review,* 86: 1019–1028.

Gledhill, Christine, ed. 1991. *Stardom: Industry of Desire.* London: Routledge.

Goertzel, Mildred George, Victor Goertzel, and Ted George Goertzel. 1978. *Three Hundred Eminent Personalities: A Psychosocial Analysis of the Famous.* San Francisco: Jossey-Bass.

Goffman, Erving. 1963. *Stigma: Notes on the Management of Spoiled Identity.* Englewood Cliffs, N.zj.: Prentice-Hall.

Goldman, Herbert G. 1991. *Banjo Eyes: Eddie Cantor and the Birth of Modern Stardom.* New York: Oxford University Press.

Goldsmith, Barbara. 1983. "The Meaning of Celebrity." *New York Times Magazine,* Dec, 4, pp. 75–82, 120.

Goode, William J. 1978. *The Celebration of Heroes: Prestige as a Social Control System.* Berkeley: University of California Press.

Goodman, Walter. 1997. "Finding It Hard to Say That Enough is Enough." *New York Times* (Washington ed.), Sept. 11, p. B6.

Gould, Stephen Jay. 1996. *Full House: The Spread of Excellence from Plato to Darwin.* New York: Harmony Books.

Gouldner, Alvin W. 1965. *Enter Plato: Classical Greece and the Origins of Social Theory.* New York; Basic Books.

Greeley, Andrew. 1991. *The Catholic Myth: The Behavior and Beliefs of American Catholics.* New York: Collier Books.

Green, Tim. 1996. *The Dark Side of the Game: My Life in the NFL.* New York: Warner Books.

Greenwald, Jeff. 1998. *Future Perfect: How Star Trek Conquered Planet Earth.* New York: Viking.

Griffin, Dustin. 1996. *Literary Patronage in England, 1650–1800.* Cambridge: Cambridge University Press.

Griffin, Jasper. 1980. *Homer on Life and Death.* Oxford: Clarendon Press.

Guinness Book of World Records, The. 1997. Stamford, Conn.: Guinness Media, 1997.

Guthrie, W. K. C. 1955. *The Greeks and Their Gods.* Boston: Beacon Press.

Guttmann, Allen. 1978. *From Ritual to Record: The Nature of Modern Sports.* New York: Columbia University Press.

———1992. *The Olympics: A History of the Modern Games.* Urbana: University of Illinois Press.

Habermas, Jürgen. 1989. *The Structural Transformation of the Public Sphere: An Inquiry into the Category of Bourgeois Society.* Cambridge: MIT Press.

Haddock, David D., and Fred S. McChesney. 1994. "Why Do Firms Contrive Shortages? The Economics of Intentional Mispricing." *Economic Inquiry,* 32: 562–581.

Hagen, Robert M. 1988. *The Breakthrough: The Race for the Superconductor.* New York: Summit Books.

Haller, Vera. 1997. "From 'Saint of the Gutters to Canonized Saint Takes Time." *Washington Post,* Sept. 14, p. A24.

Haller, William. 1963. *Foxe's Book of Martyrs and the Elect Nation.* London: Jonathan Cape.

Hamilton, James T. 1998. *Channeling Violence: The Economic Market for Violent Television Programming.* Princeton: Princeton University Press.

Hansmann, Henry. 1980. "The Role of NonProfit Enterprise." *Yale Law Journal,* 89: 835–901.

———1987. "Economic Theories of Non-Profit Organization." In *The Nonprofit Sector: A Research Handbook,* ed. Walter W. Powell, pp. 27–42. New Haven: Yale University Press.

Harrington, C. Lee, and Denise D. Bielby. 1995. *Soap Fans: Pursuing Pleasure and Making Meaning in Everyday Life.* Philadelphia: Temple University Press.

Hašek, Jaroslav. 1930. *The Good Soldier Schweik.* New York: Charles Boni.

Hauser, Thomas. 1991. *Muhammad Ali: His Life and Times.* New York: Simon and Schuster.

Havelock, Eric A. 1963. *Preface to Plato.* Oxford: Basil Blackwell.

Havill, Adrian. 1996. *Man of Steel: The Career and Courage of Christopher Reeve.* New York: Signet.

Hazlitt, William. 1948 [1814]. "Why the Arts Are Not Progressive—a Fragment." In *Selected Essays of William Hazlitt, 1778–1830,* ed. Geoffrey Keynes. London: Nonesuch Press.

Herman, Edward S., and Noam Chomsky. 1988. *Manufacturing Consent: The Political Economy of the Mass Media.* New York: Pantheon Books.

Heymann, C. David. 1989. *A Woman Named Jackie.* New York: Signet.

Hirsch, Fred. 1976. *Social Limits to Growth.* Cambridge: Harvard University Press.

Hirschman, Albert O. 1970. *Exit, Voice, and Loyalty.* Cambridge: Harvard University Press.

———1977. *The Passions and the Interests: Political Arguments for Capitalism Before Its Triumph.* Princeton: Princeton University Press.

———1989. "Having Opinions—One of the Elements of Well-Being?" *American Economic Review,* 76: 75–85.

Hobbes, Thomas. 1991 [1651]. *Levianthan.* Edited by Richard Tuck. Cambridge: Cambridge University Press.

Hoberman, John. 1997. *Darwin's Athletes: How Sport Has Damaged Black America and Preserved the Myth of Race.* Boston: Houghton Mifflin.

Hohenberg, John. 1974. *The Pulitzer Diaries: A History of the Awards in Books, Drama, Music, and Journalism, Based on the Private Files over Six Decades.* New York: Columbia University Press.

Holmes, Richard. 1985. *Acts of War: The Behavior of Men in Battle.* New York: Free Press.

Homer. 1963. *Odyssey*. Translated by Robert Fitzgerald. Garden City, N.Y.: Anchor Books.

Hume, David. 1966 [1777]. *An Enquiry Concerning the Principles of Morals*. La Salle, Ill.: Open Court Classics.

———1985 [1777]. *Essays: Moral, Political, and Literary*. Indianapolis: Liberty Classics.

———1989 [1739–1740]. *A Treatise on Human Nature*. Oxford: Clarendon Press.

Iannacconne, Laurence R. 1988. "A Formal Model of Church and Sect." In *Organizations and Institutions: Sociological and Economic Approaches to the Analysis of Social Structure*, ed. Christopher Winship and Sherwin Rosen, pp. S241—S268. Chicago: University of Chicago Press.

———1992. "Sacrifice and Stigma: Reducing Free-Riding in Cults, Communes, and Other Collectives." *Journal of Political Economy*, 100: 271–291.

Irwin-Jarecka, Iwona. 1994. *Frames of Remembrance: The Dynamics of Collective Memory*. New Brunswick, N.J.: Transaction Publishers.

James, Bill. 1988. *The Bill James Historical Baseball Abstract*. New York: Villard Books.

———1994. *The Politics of Glory*. New York: Macmillan.

James, Clive. 1993. *Fame in the Twentieth Century*. New York: Random House.

Janaway, Christopher. 1995. *Images of Excellence: Plato's Critique of the Arts*. Oxford: Clarendon Press.

Jenkins, Henry. 1991. *Textual Poachers: Television Fans and Participatory Culture*. New York: Routledge.

Johnson, Roy S. 1998. "The Jordan Effect." *Fortune*, June 22, 124–138.

Jones, George Fenwick. 1960. *Honor in German Literature*. Chapel Hill: University of North Carolina Press.

Jones, Thomas C., in collaboration with Buck Dawson. 1977. *The Halls of Fame: Featuring Specialized Museums of Sports, Agronomy, Entertainment, and the Humanities*, vols. 1–2. Chicago: J. G. Ferguson.

Juvenal. 1961. *Satires*. In *Juvenal and Persius*. Loeb Classical Library. Cambridge: Harvard University Press.

Kahneman, Daniel, P. Slovic, and Amos Tversky. 1982. *Judgment under Uncertainty: Heuristics and Biases.* Cambridge: Cambridge University Press.

Kammen, Michael. 1991. *Mystic Chords of Memory: The Transformation of Tradition in American Culture.* New York: Alfred A. Knopf.

Kanouse, D., and E. Pullan. 1981. *When Praise Impedes Performance.* New York: Rand Corporation Publications.

Kapsis, Robert E. 1989. "Reputation Building and the Film Art World: The Case of Alfred Hitchcock." *The Sociological Quarterly,* 30: 15–35.

Karger, Dave. 1998. "Tru Lives." *Entertainment Weekly,* June 12, pp. 87–88.

Katz, Leo. 1996. *Ill-Gotten Gains: Evasion, Blackmail, Fraud, and Kindred Puzzles of the Law.* Chicago: University of Chicago Press.

Kayden, Xandra. 1990. *Surviving Power: The Experience of Power—Exercising It and Giving It Up.* New York: Free Press.

Kealey, Terence. 1996. *The Economic Laws of Scientific Research.* New York: St. Martin's Press.

Kelley, Kitty. 1986. *His Way: The Unauthorized Biography of Frank Sinatra.* New York: Bantam Books.

Kellner, Douglas. 1992. *The Persian Gulf TV War.* Boulder: Westview Press.

Kemp, Eric Waldram. 1948. *Canonization and Authority in the Western Church.* London: Oxford University Press.

Kernan, Alvin. 1987. *Samuel Johnson and the Impact of Print.* Princeton: Princeton University Press.

Kiernan, V. G. 1988. *The Duel in European History: Honour and the Reign of Aristocracy.* Oxford: Oxford University Press.

Klapp, Orrin E. 1964. *Symbolic Leaders: Public Dramas and Public Men.* Chicago: Aldine.

——1991. *Inflation of Symbols: Loss of Values in American Culture.* New Brunswick, N.J.: Transaction Publishers.

Klein, Benjamin, and Keith Leffler. 1981. "The Role of Market Forces in Assuring Contractual Performance." *Journal of Political Economy,* 89: 615–641.

Klein, Daniel B., ed. 1997. *Reputation: Studies in the Voluntary Elicitation of Good Conduct.* Ann Arbor, Mich.: University of Michigan Press.

Kleinberg, Aviad M. 1992. *Prophets in Their Own Country: Living Saints and the Making of Sainthood in the Later Middle Ages.* Chicago: University of Chicago Press.

Kojève, Alexandre. 1969. *Introduction to the Reading of Hegel.* New York: Basic Books.

Koonce, B. G. 1966. *Chaucer and the Tradition of Fame: Symbolism in The House of Fame.* Princeton: Princeton University Press.

Kostelanetz, Richard. 1973. *The End of Intelligent Writing.* New York: Sheed and Ward.

Kuran, Timur. 1995. *Private Truths, Public Lies: The Social Consequences of Preference Falsification.* Cambridge: Harvard University Press.

Kurtz, Howard. 1996. *Hot Air: All Talk, All the Time.* New York: Random House.

Kydland, Finn E., and Edward Prescott. 1977. "Rules Rather Than Discretion: The Inconsistency of Optimal Plans." *Journal of Political Economy*, 1977, 85: 473–492.

Labaton, Stephen. 1997. "U. S. Tells Court Microsoft Breaks Antitrust Accord." *New York Times* (Washington ed.), TOct. 21, pp. A1, D22.

Landes, William M., and Richard A. Posner. 1987. "Trademark Law: An Economic Perspective." *Journal of Law and Economics*, 30: 265–309.

Lang, Gladys Engel, and Kurt Lang. 1988. "Recognition and Renown: The Survival and Artistic Reputation." *American Journal of Sociology*, 94: 79–109.

——— 1990. *Etched in Memory: The Building and Survival of Artistic Reputation.* Chapel Hill: University of North Carolina Press.

Larson, Jennifer. 1995. *Greek Heroine Cults.* Madison: University of Wisconsin Press.

Leibovich, Mark. 1999. "A Familiar Voice on the Phone." *Washington Post*, Jan.13, pp. A1, A16.

Levine, Madeline. 1996. *Viewing Violence: How Media Violence Affects Your Child's and Adolescent's Development.* New York: Doubleday.

Levy, David. 1992. *The Economic Ideas of Ordinary People*. London: Routledge.

Lewis, Michael. 1998. *World Cup Soccer*. London: Moyer Bell.

Lida de Malkiel, Maria Rosa. 1983. *La Idea de la Fama en la Edad Media Castellana*. Mexico: Fondo de Cultural Económica.

Livingston, Jane, and Jane Beardsley. 1982. *Black Folk Art in America, 1930–1980*. Jackson: University of Mississippi Press.

Locke, John. 1989 [1693]. *Some Thoughts Concerning Education*. Oxford: Clarendon Press.

Longinus. 1985. *On the Sublime*. Translated with commentary by James A. Arieti and John M. Crossett. New York: The Edwin Mellen Press.

Lovejoy, Arthur O. 1961. *Reflections on Human Nature*. Baltimore: The Johns Hopkins University Press.

Lowenthal, David. 1985. *The Past Is a Foreign Country*. Cambridge: Cambridge University Press.

————1996. *Possessed by the Past: The Heritage Crusade and the Spoils of History*. New York: The Free Press.

Lowenthal, Leo. 1956. "Biographies in Popular Magazines." In *American Social Patterns*, ed. William Petersen, pp. 63–118. New York: Doubleday Anchor Books.

————1961. *Literature, Popular Culture, and Society*. Palo Alto, Calif.: Pacific Books.

Lubin, Harold. 1968. *Heroes and Anti-Heroes: A Reader in Depth*. San Francisco: Chandler.

Luckinbill, D. 1977. "Criminal Homicide as a Situated Transaction." *Social Problems*, 25: 176–186.

Lyall, Sarah. 1997. "Diana's Hunters: How Quarry Was Stalked." *New York Times* (Washington ed.), Sept. 10, pp. A1, A10.

Lyons, Deborah. 1997. *Gender and Immortality: Heroines and Ancient Greek Myth and Cult*. Princeton: Princeton University Press.

McAdams, Richard H. 1992. "Relative Preferences." *The Yale Law Journal*, 102: 1–104.

McCann, Graham. 1996. *Cary Grant: A Class Apart*. New York: Columbia University Press.

McCloskey, Donald N. 1994. *Knowledge and Persuasion in Economics.* Cambridge: Cambridge University Press.

McCracken, Grant. 1989. "Who Is the Celebrity Endorser? Cultural Foundations of the Endorsement Process." *Journal of Consumer Research,* 16: 310–321.

McDonald, Forrest. 1994. *The American Presidency: An Intellectual History.* Lawrence: University Press of Kansas.

Macken, Rev. Thomas F. 1910. *The Canonisation of Saints.* Dublin: M. H. Gill & Son.

MacMillan, James. 1969. *The Honours Game.* London: Leslie Frewin.

Maizels, John. 1996. *Raw Creation: Outsider Art and Beyond.* London: Phaidon Press.

Makkai, Toni, and John Braithwaite. 1993. "Praise, Price and Corporate Compliance." *International Journal of the Sociology of Law,* 21: 73–91.

Maland, Charles J. 1989. *Chaplin and American Culture: The Evolution of a Star Image.* Princeton: Princeton University Press.

Mandeville, Bernard. 1988 [1735]. *The Fable of the Bees, or Private Vices, Publick Benefits.* Indianapolis: Liberty Classics.

Maresca, Frank, and Roger Ricco, with Lyle Rexer. 1993. *American Self-Taught: Paintings and Drawings by Outsider Artists.* New York: Alfred A. Knopf.

Margolis, Susan. 1977. *Fame.* San Francisco: San Francisco Book Co.

Mariana, Juan de. 1948 [1599]. *The King and the Education of the King.* Translated by George Albert Moore. Chevy Chase, Md.: The Country Dollar Press.

Marler, Regina. 1997. *Bloomsbury Pie: The Making of the Bloomsbury Boom.* New York: Henry Holt.

Marsh, Dave. 1985. *Trapped: Michael Jackson and the Crossover Dream.* New York: Bantam Books.

Marshall, P. David. 1997. *Celebrity and Power: Fame in Contemporary Culture.* Minneapolis: University of Minnesota Press.

Medved, Michael. 1992. *Hollywood vs. America: Popular Culture and the War on Traditional Values.* New York: HarperCollins.

Melman, Yossi. 1992. *The New Israelis: An Intimate View of a Changing People.* New York: Birch Lane Press.

Mercer, Jonathan. 1996. *Reputation and International Politics.* Ithaca: Cornell University Press.

"Merged Book Market The." 1998. *Washington Post Book World,* April 12, p. 15.

Merkelbach, R. 1967. "Die Heroen als Geber des Guten und Bösen." *Zeitschrift für Papyrologie und Epigraphik,* 1 (2): 97–99.

Merton, Robert K. 1973. *The Sociology of Science: Theoretical and Empirical Investigations.* Chicago: University of Chicago Press.

Meyer, Karl E. 1997. "How Fickle Fortune and Men's Eyes." *New York Times* (Washington ed.), Nov. 15, pp. B7–8.

Meyrowitz, Joshua. 1985. *No Sense of Place: The Impact of Electronic Media on Social Behavior.* New York: Oxford University Press.

Mikalson, Jon D. 1991. *Honor Thy Gods: Popular Religion in Greek Tragedy.* Chapel Hill: University of North Carolina Press.

Mill, John Stuart. 1950 [1838]. *On Bentham and Coleridge.* New York: Harper Torchbooks.

Milton, Joyce. 1993. *Loss of Eden: A Biography of Charles and Anne Morrow Lindbergh.* New York: HarperCollins.

Mitroff, Ian I., and Warren Bennis. 1989. *The Unreality Industry: The Deliberate Manufacturing of Falsehood and What It Is Doing to Our Lives.* New York: Oxford University Press.

Monaco, James. 1978. *Celebrity: The Media as Image Makers.* New York: Dell Publishing.

Montaigne, Michel de. 1967. *Complete Works of Montaigne.* Edited by Donald M. Frame. Stanford: Stanford University Press.

Morgan, Peter W., and Glenn H. Reynolds. 1997. *The Appearance of Impropriety: How the Ethics Wars Have Undermined American Government, Business, and Society.* New York: Free Press.

Mulkay, Michael, and Elizabeth Chaplin. 1982. "Aesthetics and the Artistic Career: A Study of Anomie in Fine-Art Painting." *The Sociological Quarterly,* 23: 117–138.

Nagel, Thomas. 1995. *Other Minds: Critical Essays, 1969–1994.* New York: Oxford University Press.

Nagy, Gregory. 1979. *The Best of the Achaeans: Concepts of the Hero in Archaic Greek Poetry.* Baltimore: The Johns Hopkins University Press.

Neapolitan, Jerry. 1988. "The Effects of Different Types of Praise and Criticism on Performance." *Sociological Focus,* 21: 223–231.

Nelson, Philip. 1974. "Advertising as Information." *Journal of Political Economy,* 82: 729–754.

Neuborne, Ellen. 1998. "This Call Brought to You By . . ." *Business Week,* June 29, p. 8.

Nilsson, Martin P. 1964. *A History of Greek Religion.* New York: W. W. Norton.

1997 Fan Club Directory, The. 1997. Burbank, Calif.: National Association of Fan Clubs.

Nisbett, Richard E., and Dov Cohen. 1996. *Culture of Honor: The Psychology of Violence in the South.* Boulder: Westview Press.

Ohanian, Roobina. 1990. "Construction and Validation of a Scale to Measure Celebrity Endorsers' Perceived Expertise, Trustworthiness, and Attractiveness." *Journal of Advertising,* 3: 39–52.

O'Neal, Sean. 1996. *Elvis, Inc.: The Fall and Rise of the Presley Empire.* Rocklin, Calif.: Prims Publishing.

Orvell, Miles. 1995. *After the Machine: Visual Arts and the Erasing of Cultural Boundaries.* Jackson: University of Mississippi Press.

Ostrower, Francis. 1995. *Why the Wealthy Give: The Culture of Elite Philanthropy.* Princeton: Princeton University Press.

Ostwald, Peter. 1997. *Glenn Gould: The Ecstasy and Tragedy of Genius.* New York: W. W. Norton.

Owen, Bruce M., and Steven S. Wildman. 1992. *Video Economics.* Cambridge: Harvard University Press.

Paik, Haejung, and George Comstock. 1994. "The Effects of Television Violence on Antisocial Behavior: A Meta-Analysis." *Communication Research,* 21: 516–546.

Parenti, Michael. 1992. *Make-Believe Media: The Politics of Entertainment.* New York: St. Martin's Press.

———1993. *Inventing: The Politics of News Media Reality.* New York: St. Martin's Press.

Pascal, Blaise. 1995 [1670]. *Pensées.* London: Penguin.

Patalas, Enno. 1963. *Sozialgeschichte der Stars.* Hamburg: Marion von Schroeder Verlag.

Pattison, Robert. 1987. *The Triumph of Vulgarity: Rock Music in the Mirror of Romanticism.* New York: Oxford University Press.

Paulson, Ronald. 1989. *Breaking and Remaking: Aesthetic Practice in England, 1700–1820.* New Brunswick, N.J.: Rutgers University Press.

Pettit, Philip. 1990. "*Virtus Normativa:* Rational Choice Perspectives." *Ethics,* 100: 725–755.

Petrarch. 1962. *The Triumphs of Petrarch.* Translated by Ernest Hatch Wilkins. Chicago: University of Chicago Press.

Phillips, Michael M. 1997. "Taking Stock: Top Sports Pros Find a New Way to Score: Getting Equity Stakes." *Wall Street Journal,* April 18, pp. A1, A8.

Plato. 1956. *Symposium.* In *The Works of Plato,* ed. Irwin Edman, pp. 333–393. New York: Modern Library.

Plato. 1968. *The Republic.* In *The Republic of Plato,* tran. and ed. Allan Bloom. New York: Basic Books.

Plotnik, Arthur. 1996. *The Elements of Expression: Putting Thoughts into Words.* New York: Henry Holt.

Plutarch. n.d. *The Lives of the Noble Grecians and Romans.* New York: Modern Library.

———1957. "Flattery and Friendship." In *On Love, the Family, and the Good Life, Selected Essays of Plutarch.* Translated and edited by Moses Hadas. New York: Mentor Books, pp. 123–165.

———1993. *Selected Essays and Dialogues.* Oxford: Oxford University Press.

Podolny, Joel M. 1993. "A Status-Based Model of Market Competition." *American Journal of Sociology,* 98: 829–872.

"Popcorn Tins, Aprons, Valentines, and Bandages All Look like Mike." 1996. *Wall Street Journal,* Nov. 15, p. B1.

Pope, Alexander. 1966 [1715]. "The Temple of Fame." In *The Poems of Alexander Pope,* vol. 2, ed. Geoffrey Tillotson, pp. 253–289. London: Methuen.

Posner, Richard A. 1981. *The Economics of Justice.* Cambridge: Harvard University Press.

———1990. *Cardozo: A Study in Reputation.* Chicago: University of Chicago Press.

"Public Television: The Taxpayer's Wagner." 1992. *The Economist*, May 30, p. 41.

Quebedeaux, Richard. 1982. *By What Authority: The Rise of Personality Cults in American Christianity.* San Francisco: Harper & Row.

Quiller-Couch, Arthur T. 1911. *The Roll Call of Honour: A New Book of Golden Deeds.* London: Thomas Nelson and Sons.

Rader, Benjamin G. 1984. *In Its Own Image: How Television Transformed Sports.* New York: Free Press.

Raeburn, John. 1984. *Fame Became of Him: Hemingway as Public Writer.* Bloomington: Indiana University Press.

Rearick, Charles. 1997. *The French in Love and War: Popular Culture in the Era of the World Wars.* New Haven: Yale University Press.

Reid, Robert H. 1997. *Architects of the Web: One Thousand Days that Built the Future of Business.* New York: John Wiley & Sons.

Rein, Irving J., Philip Kotler, and Martin R. Stoller. 1987. *High Visibility.* New York: Dodd, Mead.

Reissland, Nadja. 1994. "The Socialisation of Pride in Young Children." *International Journal of Behavioral Development*, 17: 541–552.

Rich, Frank. 1998. "What the Tube Is For." *New York Times Magazine,* Sept. 20, pp. 53–56.

Riding, Alan. 1997. "Public Likes Celebrity Photos But Hates the Photographers." *New York Times* (Washington ed.), Sept. 2, pp. A1, A11.

Roche, George. 1987. *A World without Heroes: The Modern Tragedy.* Hillsdale, Mich.: Hillsdale College Press.

Rodden, John. 1989. *The Politics of Literary Reputation: The Making and the Claiming of "St. George" Orwell.* New York: Oxford University Press.

Rodman, Gilbert B. 1996. *Elvis After Elvis: The Posthumous Career of a Living Legend.* London: Routledge.

Rosen, Sherwin. 1981. "The Economics of Superstars." *American Economic Review,* 68: 845–858.

Rosenfeld, Megan. 1998. "Van Gogh's Drawing Power." *Washington Post,* Sept. 20, pp. A1, A12.

Rossi-Landi, Ferruccio. 1983. *Language as Work and Trade: A Semiotic Homology for Linguistics and Economics.* South Hadley, Mass.: Bergin & Garvey.

Rothmyer, Karen. 1991. *Winning Pulitzers: The Stories behind Some of the Best News Coverage of Our Time.* New York: Columbia University Press.

Rousseau, Jean-Jacques. 1968 [1758]. *Politics and the Arts: Letter to M. D'Alembert on the Theatre.* Ithaca: Cornell University Press.

Russell, Gordon W. 1993. *The Social Psychology of Sport.* New York: Springer-Verlag.

Ryle, John. 1996. "Gaze of Power." *Guardian*, Jan. 12, sect. 2, p. 3, col. 4.

Sabato, Larry J. 1991. *Feeding Frenzy: How Attack Journalism Has Transformed American Politics.* New York: Free Press.

Salisbury, Harrison E. 1993. *Heroes of My Time.* New York: Walker and Company.

Sammons, Jeffrey T. 1988. *Beyond the Ring: The Role of Boxing in American Society.* Urbana: University of Illinois Press.

Sandford, Christopher. 1995. *Kurt Cobain.* New York: Carroll and Graf Publishers.

Sanello, Frank. 1997. *Jimmy Stewart: A Wonderful Life.* New York: Kensington Publishing Corp.

Sanjek, Russell. 1988. *American Popular Music and Its Business. The First Four Hundred Years,* vol. 3: *From 1900 to 1984.* New York: Oxford University Press.

Scharfstein, David S., and Jeremy C. Stein. 1990. "Herd Behavior and Investment." *American Economic Review*, 80: 465–479.

Scheffer, John D. 1936. "The Idea of Decline in Literature and the Fine Arts in Eighteenth-Century England." *Modern Philology*, 34: 155–178.

Schein, Seth. 1984. *The Mortal Hero: An Introduction to Homer's "Iliad."* Berkeley: University of California Press.

Schelling, Thomas C. 1960. *The Strategy of Conflict.* Cambridge: Harvard University Press.

———1984. *Choice and Consequence.* Cambridge: Harvard University Press.

Schickel, Richard. 1973. *His Picture in the Papers: A Speculation on Celebrity in America Based on the Life of Douglas Fairbanks, Sr.* New York: Charterhouse.

———1985. *Intimate Strangers: The Culture of Celebrity.* New York: Doubleday.

Schiller, Herbert. 1989. *Culture, Inc.: The Corporate Takeover of Public Expression.* New York: Oxford University Press.

Schlesinger, Arthur. 1961. "The Decline of Heroes." In *Adventures of the Mind,* ed. Richard Thruelson and John Kobler, pp. 95–106. New York: Alfred A. Knopf.

Schopenhauer, Arthur. 1936. "The Wisdom of Life." In *The Philosophy of Arthur Schopenhauer,* ed. and trans.Belfort Bax and Bailey Saunders, pp. 3–100. New York: Tudor Publishing.

———1960 [1851]. *The Art of Literature.* Ann Arbor, Mich.: University of Michigan Press.

Schor, Juliet. 1996. "What's Wrong with Consumer Capitalism? *The Joyless Economy* after Twenty Years." *Critical Review,* 10: 495–508.

Schwartz, Barry. 1987. *George Washington: The Making of an American Symbol.* New York: Free Press.

Scott 1995 Specialized Catalogue of United States Stamps. 1994. Sidney, Ohio: Scott Publishing.

Semple, Janet. 1993. *Bentham's Prison.* Oxford: Clarendon Press.

Seneca. 1962. *Ad Lucilium Epistulae Morales [Epistles],* 3 vols. Cambridge: Harvard University Press.

Shakespeare, William. 1957. *Othello.* New York: Washington Square Press.

———1961. *Antony and Cleopatra.* New York: Washington Square Press.

———1961. *Henry IV, Part II.* New York: Washington Square Press.

———1972. *The Tragedy of Richard the Second.* New York: Washington Square Press.

———1989. *Henry VI, Parts One, Two, and Three.* New York: Signet Classics.

———1994. *Henry IV, Part I.* New York: Washington Square Press.

———1995. *Henry V.* New York: Washington Square Press.

Shales, Tom. 1992. "A Myopic '20/20': John Lennon's Killer Gets Star Treatment." *Washington Post,* Dec. 4, pp. D1, D6.

Shalit, Wendy. 1999. *A Return to Modesty: Discovering the Lost Virtue.* New York: Free Press.

Shea, Christopher. 1998. "Shopping Malls and 'Armageddon' as Triumphs of the Human Spirit." *The Chronicle of Higher Education,* July 24, pp. A13-A14.

Shenon, Philip. 1996. "What's a Medal Worth Today?" *New York Times,* May 26, p. E5.

Shrum, Wesley Monroe, Jr. 1996. *Fringe and Fortune: The Role of Critics in High and Popular Art.* Princeton: Princeton University Press.

Silk, Michael. 1987. *Homer: "The Iliad."* Cambridge: Cambridge University Press.

Smith, Adam. 1937 [1776]. *An Inquiry into the Nature and Causes of the Wealth of Nations.* New York: The Modern Library.

———1981 [1759]. *Theory of Moral Sentiments.* Indianapolis: Liberty Press Classics.

Smith, Janna Malamud. 1997. *Private Matters: In Defense of the Personal Life.* New York: Addison-Wesley.

Smith, Ken. 1982. *Baseball's Hall of Fame.* New York: Grosset and Dunlap.

Smith, Ronald L. 1997. *Cosby: The Life of a Comedy Legend.* Amherst, N.Y.: Prometheus Books.

Soderberg, Paul, Helen Washington,and Jaques Cattell Press. 1977. *The Big Book of Halls of Fame in the United States and Canada,* vol. 1. New York: Bowker.

Spence, A. Michael. 1974. *Market Signaling: Informational Transfer in Hiring and Related Screening Processes.* Cambridge: Harvard University Press.

Spinoza, Benedict. 1951. "On the Improvement of the Understanding." In *The Chief Works of Benedict de Spinoza.* New York: Dover Publications.

Spoto, Donald. 1993. *Marilyn Monroe: The Biography.* New York: Harper Paperbacks.

———1995. *The Decline and Fall of the House of Windsor.* New York: Pocket Books.

References

Springwood, Charles Fruehling. 1996. *Cooperstown to Dyersville: A Geography of Baseball Nostalgia.* Boulder: Westview Press.

Stack, Steven. 1987. "Celebrities and Suicide: A Taxonomy and Analysis, 1948–1983." *American Sociological Review,* 40: 401–412.

Starker, Steven. 1989. *Evil Influences: Crusades against the Mass Media.* New Brunswick, N.J.: Transaction Publishers.

Steinmetz, Greg. 1996. "Andy Warhol Finds at Least Fifteen Minutes of Fame in Slovakia." *Wall Street Journal,* April 26, pp. A1, A6.

Stephan, Paula E., and Sharon G. Levin. 1992. *Striking the Mother Lode in Science: The Importance of Age, Place, and Time.* New York: Oxford University Press.

Stewart, Frank Henderson. 1994. *Honor.* Chicago: University of Chicago Press.

Strauss, Neil. 1998. "Restless Music Fans Hungry for the New." *New York Times,* Jan. 28, pp. E1, E7.

———1999. "The Price of Fame Includes Dinner." *New York Times,* Jan. 13, pp. B1, B3.

Stuhlhofer, Franz. 1987. *Lohn und Strafe in der Wissenschaft.* Vienna: Böhlau Verlag.

"Style Invitational, The." 1997. *Washington Post,* Nov. 9, p. F2.

Sudjic, Deyan. 1990. *Cult Heroes: How to Be Famous for More Than Fifteen Minutes.* New York: W. W. Norton.

Sutter, Daniel. 1998. "Media Scrutiny and the Quality of Politicians." Unpublished ms. University of Oklahoma.

Swift, Jonathan. 1958. *"Gulliver's Travels" and Other Writings.* New York: Random House.

Tagliabue, John. 1997. "Europe Offering Free Calls, But First, a Word from . . ." New York Times (Washington ed.), Sept. 28, pp. A1, A8.

Taylor, Gary. 1996. *Cultural Selection.* New York: Basic Books.

Temkin, Larry S. 1993. *Inequality.* New York: Oxford University Press.

Tenner, Edward. 1996. *Why Things Bite Back: Technology and the Revenge of Unintended Consequences.* New York: Alfred A. Knopf.

Thaler, Paul. 1997. *The Spectacle: Media and the Making of the O. J. Simpson Story.* Westport, Conn.: Praeger.

Thiele, Leslie Paul. 1990. *Friedrich Nietzsche and the Politics of the Soul.* Princeton: Princeton University Press.

Thigpen, David E. 1998. "Is That a Song or a Sales Pitch?" *Time,* Aug. 3, p. 73.

Thorn, John, and Pete Palmer, with David Reuther. 1984. *The Hidden Game of Baseball: A Revolutionary Approach to Baseball and Its Statistics.* Garden City, N.Y.: Doubleday.

Thurow, Roger. 1997. "Lots of Affection: To See Why the NFL Still Thrives, Consider Jersey John's Odysseys." *Wall Street Journal,* Oct. 10, p. A1.

Tillotson, Geoffrey. 1966. "Introduction to Pope's 'The Temple of Fame.'" In *The Poems of Alexander Pope,* vol. 2, pp. 215–244. London: Methuen.

Tirole, Jean. 1996. "A Theory of Collective Reputations (with Applications to the Persistence of Corruption and to Firm Quality)." *Review of Economic Studies,* 63: 1–22.

Tocqueville, Alexis de. 1969 [1835]. *Democracy in America.* New York: Harper & Row.

Todd, Richard. 1996. *Consuming Fictions: The Booker Prize and Fiction in Britain Today.* London: Bloomsbury.

Tompkins, Jane. 1984. "Masterpiece Theater: The Politics of Hawthorne's Literary Reputation." *American Quarterly,* 36: 617–642.

Turner, Richard. 1990. *In Your Blood: Football Culture in the Late 1980's and Early 1990's.* Working Press.

Twitchell, James B. 1996. *Adcult USA: The Triumph of Advertising in American Culture.* New York: Columbia University Press.

———*For Shame: The Loss of Common Decency in American Culture.* New York: St. Martin's Press.

"Unsafe at Any Megahertz." 1997. *The Economist,* Oct. 11, p. 80.

Valhouli, Constantine Archimedes. 1998. "Taking Care of Business: Managing the Death and Legacy of Celebrity Musicians." Master's thesis, Georgetown University.

Vermoral, Fred, and Judy Vermoral. 1985. *Starlust: The Secret Life of Fans.* London: W. H. Allen.

Vickers, Brian. 1988. *In Defense of Rhetoric.* Oxford: Clarendon Press.

Virgil. 1985. *The Aeneid*. Translated by Robert Fitzgerald. New York: Vintage Books.

Wagner, Philip. 1996. *Showing Off: The Geltung Hypothesis*. Austin: University of Texas Press.

Watson, Curtis Brown. 1960. *Shakespeare and the Renaissance Concept of Honor*. Princeton: Princeton University Press.

Waxman, Sharon. 1997. "Golden Globes' New Spin: Hollywood Press Group Admits Problems." *Washington Post*, Dec. 18, pp. C1, C14.

Weeks, Linton. 1998. "Dead Reckoning: They Bet on Which Celebrity Will Die Next." *Washington Post*, Jan. 11, pp. F1, F4.

Weigelt, Keith, and Colin Camerer. 1988. "Reputation and Corporate Strategy: A Review of Recent Theory and Applications." *Strategic Management Journal*, 9: 443–454.

Weil, Simone. 1952. *The Need for Roots: Prelude to a Declaration of Duties toward Mankind*. Boston: Beacon Press.

———1983. "The Iliad or The Poem of Force." In *Revisions: Changing Perspectives in Moral Philosophy*, ed Stanley Hauerwas and Alasdair MacIntyre, pp. 222–248.Notre Dame, Ind.: University of Notre Dame Press

Weinstein, Deena. 1991. *Heavy Metal: A Cultural Sociology*. New York: Lexington Books.

Wertham, Fredric. 1973. *The World of Fanzines: A Special Form of Communication*. Carbondale: Southern Illinois University Press.

Westie, Frank R. 1973. "Academic Expectations of Professional Immortality: A Study of Legitimation." *The American Sociologist*, 8: 19–32.

Whitburn, Joel. 1997. *Billboard Top 1000 Singles, 1955–1996*. Milwaukee: Hal Leonard Corporation.

Wilbon, Michael. 1998. "Jordan Steers, Bulls Win." *Washington Post*, June 15, pp. A1, A12.

Wilford, John Noble. 1996. "Did Byrd Reach Pole? His Diary Hints 'No.'" *New York Times*, May 6, pp. A1, B10.

Williamson, Roxanne Kuter. 1991. *American Architects and the Mechanics of Fame*. Austin: University of Texas Press.

Wills, Geoff, and Cary L. Cooper. 1988. *Pressure Sensitive: Popular Musicians under Stress.* London: Sage Publications.

Wilson, Sir Arnold, and Capt. J. H. F. McEwen. 1939. *Gallantry: Its Public Recognition and Reward in Peace and in War at Home and Abroad.* London: Oxford University Press.

Windeler, Robert. 1973. *Sweetheart: The Story of Mary Pickford.* New York: Praeger Publishers.

Wise, Mike. 1998. "As the Stars in the N. B. A. Rise, the League's Level of Play Falls." *New York Times,* Feb, 8, pp. A1, A18.

Woodward, Kenneth L. 1990. *Making Saints: How the Catholic Church Determines Who Becomes a Saint, Who Doesn't, and Why.* New York: Simon and Schuster.

World Dictionary of Awards and Prizes. 1979. London: Europa Publications.

Wyatt-Brown, Bertram. 1986. *Honor and Violence in the Old South.* New York: Oxford University Press.

Young, Edward. 1906 [1726–1728]. "Love of Fame, the Universal Passion." In *The Poetical Works of Edward Young,* vol. 2, pp. 59–140. London: George Bell and Sons.

Yutang, Lin, ed. 1949. *The Wisdom of Laotse.* New York: Random House.

Zachary, G. Pascal. 1997. "CEOs Are Stars Now, But Why? And Would Alfred Sloan Approve?" *Wall Street Journal,* Sept. 3, pp. A1, A8.

Zha, Jianying. 1995. *China Pop: How Soap Operas, Tabloids, and Bestsellers Are Transforming a Culture.* New York: New Press.

Zuckerman, Harriet. 1977. *Scientific Elite: Nobel Laureates in the United States.* New York: Free Press.

Zwiebel, Jeffrey. 1995. "Corporate Conservatism and Relative Compensation." *Journal of Political Economy,* 103: 1–25.

Acknowledgments

My greatest intellectual debt is to David Levy, who stimulated my interest in fame and offered useful comments and discussions throughout the preparation of the manuscript. His book *The Economic Ideas of Ordinary People* convinced me that economics can and should address the topic of fame. Without David this book would not have been written.

Conversations with Marvin Becker have been particularly valuable as well, especially for setting the book in a broader context. The editorial direction of Michael Aronson has, once again, proved extremely helpful in the development of this book. Timur Kuran read through the whole manuscript and offered many useful comments. The comments of Robert Frank have been especially helpful. Frances Cairncross of *The Economist* and John McLaughlin provided advance publicity. In addition, I wish to thank Sahar Akhtar, Meyer Burstein, Penelope Brook, Bryan Caplan, Francis Fukuyama, Diego Gambetta, Amihai Glazer, Kevin Grier, John Hall, Anna Harvey, Claire Hill, Linda Howe, Gordon Kato, Maureen Kelley, Daniel Klein, Randall

Kroszner, Thomas Schelling, Paul Smith, Dan Sutter, Alex Tabarrok, Bob Tollison, Roger Trilling, Nicola Tynan, numerous George Mason University seminar participants, seminar participants at All Soul's College, Oxford, seminar participants at the Liberty Fund conference "Shame, Fame, and Liberty," for helpful comments and conversations.

During the writing of this book I received financial assistance from the Institute of Humane Studies and the Mercatus Center at George Mason University, for which I am very grateful.

Index

137, 144–146, 150–151, 163,
167
addictive nature of, 157–161
Christian view of, 67
diversity resulting from, 164
illusions and delusions,
152–157
motives for, 1, 2, 6, 127–129,
154
political, 170
praise for sale and, 61
role models and heroes and,
47
Fan clubs, 15
Fandom/fans, 2–3, 5, 8,
153–154
celebrity endorsements and,
41–42
collective aspect of, 3, 8,
14–16, 16–22, 43, 123
control by, 39–40, 59, 60–61,
64, 70, 158, 159
conventions of, 3, 22
diversity of taste and, 103,
104, 112
exclusivity and loyalty of,
22–25
fame production and,
114–116
focal points and coordination
of, 16, 42, 43–44, 165
gatekeeper critics and, 87
hostility of, 5–6, 158, 159
organization of, 117
overcrowding and, 8
pathology of, 168
payola and, 37–38

separation of fame from merit
and, 36–37, 58–59
snowball effects of, 14–16
subscription finance and,
39–40
as substitute for participation,
6, 55
supply of fame and, 113–114,
120
unwelcome attention by, 5–6,
130–133
Fashion models, 4
Faulkner, William, 81, 165
Fermi, Enrico, 122
First Amendment rights, 165
Fischer, Bobby, 108
Fisher, Irving, 35
Flack, Roberta, 104
Fleetwood Mac, 103
Focal points and coordination,
17–18, 19, 22, 165
family identities and, 21
of fandom, 42, 43–44
publicity and, 38, 41, 42
violence and aggression and,
18–19, 70
Fonda, Jane, 4
Fonda family, 21
Ford, Gerald, 50
Ford, Harrison, 7
Ford, Henry, 57
Foreman, George, 117, 119
Forster, E. M., 85
Foster, Jodie, 2
Fowles, Jib, 151
Fox, Michael J., 132
Foxe, John, 107

Foxx, Jimmie, 111, 126
Frank, Robert H., 102, 105–106, 107
Fraud, 144–146
Frazier, Joe, 117, 119
Freed, Alan, 27
Freud, Sigmund, 89
Friedman, Milton, 35
Fry, Roger, 85
Furet, François, 36

Gable, Clark, 132
Galbraith, John Kenneth, 44–45
Garland, Judy, 22
Gatekeeper critics, 10, 72–78, 79, 80
  biases of, 81–87
  citation practices, 87–92
  conservative attitudes of, 86–87, 88, 90–91, 92
  debasement of fame and, 95
  See also Criticism/critics
Gatekeeper institutions, 72–73, 83
  long- and short-term celebrity and, 77–78
  standards for, 73–77, 85
Gates, Bill, 57, 75
Gauguin, Paul, 138
Gault-Milleau guides, 77
Gehrig, Lou, 126
General Mills, 42
General Theory (Keynes), 35
Genres, 80
George V, King, 52
Gerard, Alexander, 128
Ghoul Pool, 5

Gini coefficient, 107
Giotto, 81
Girard, Joe, 145–146
Gluck, Christoph Willibald von, 21, 71
Goethe, Johann Wolfgang, 81, 127
Golden Globe awards, 26
Goldie, 24
Gone with the Wind (film), 79
Good Soldier Schweik, The (Hašek), 146
Gordy, Berry, 92
Gould, Glenn, 5, 138
Grable, Betty, 48
Graceland, 7, 20. *See also* Presley, Elvis
Graf, Steffi, 133
Grammy Awards, 115
Grant, Cary, 4
Grant, Duncan, 85
Graves, Michael, 41
Green, Tim, 131
Greenberg, Clement, 27
Gregory, Dick, 4
Gretry, André, 71
Gretzky, Wayne, 41, 116
Griffey, Ken, 110
Griffin, Ralph, 135
Grisham, John, 79
Grove, Lefty, 117, 126
Guevara, Che, 20
Guinness Book of World Records, The, 116

Habermas, Jürgen, 10, 167
Hall, Arsenio, 51

Hall of Fame for Great
Americans, 7
Halls of Fame, 7, 72, 73, 74–75,
77, 80, 83, 86, 97, 114–115,
129. See also Baseball Hall
of Fame; Fame-producing
institutions; Rock and Roll
Hall of Fame
Hard Copy (television program),
152
Hašek, Jaroslav, 146
Hawking, Stephen, 19, 154
Haydn, Franz Joseph, 71,
120
Hazlitt, William, 127–128
Hegel, Georg, 153
Hemingway, Ernest, 19
Hendrix, Jimi, 20
Henwood, Doug, 25
Hepburn, Katharine, 1
Hill, Grant, 153
Hillary, Sir Edmund, 129
Hinckley, John, 2
Hirsch, Fred, 113
Hirschman, Albert, 55
Hobbes, Thomas, 56, 66–67,
169–170
Holly, Buddy, 20, 48
Homer, 10, 13
Homosexuality, 21–22
Hooke, Robert, 1
Hoosiers (film), 125
Hornsby, Rogers, 111
Hostility. *See* Violence and
aggression
House of Fame (Chaucer), 156
Hoyt, Waite, 126

Hume, David, 2, 127, 133, 163,
167

Iacocca, Lee, 4
I Hate Madonna Jokebook, The
(West), 5
Il Guercino, 71
Iliad (Homer), 150
Indiana High School Athletic
Association, 125
Innovation, 85, 86, 87, 89, 128,
136, 140, 141, 144. *See also*
Risk-taking behavior
In Praise of Commercial Culture
(Cowen), 11
International Institute for
Refrigeration, 115
Internet, 39
Ives, Charles, 165

Jackson, Michael, 29, 41, 102,
103, 104
Jagger, Mick, 31. *See also* Rolling
Stones
James, Bill, 75, 117
James, Henry, 21, 81
James, William, 21
Jefferson, Thomas, 64, 166
Jesus Christ, 48, 52
Joe Palooka comic strip, 48
John Paul II, Pope, 94
Johns, Jasper, 9, 31, 81
Johnson, Ben, 119
Johnson, Don, 48
Johnson, Magic, 20, 109, 119, 123
Johnson, Samuel, 118
Jones, Ernest, 89

Jordan, Michael, 7, 41, 42–43, 44, 63, 108–109, 123, 165
Joyce, James, 19, 81

Kaat, Jim, 75
Kafka, Franz, 35
Kahlo, Frida, 82
Kames, Lord, 128
Kant, Emmanuel, 167
Karpov, Anatoly, 126
Kasparov, Gary, 126
Kauffmann, Angelika, 71
Keller, Helen, 47
Kennedy, John F., 20, 50, 87
Kennedy family, 21
Keynes, John Maynard, 35, 85
Killebrew, Harmon, 118
Kosinski, Jerzy, 89
Kroszner, Randall, 97
Kubrick, Stanley, 132
Kuran, Timur, 14

Language
  privatization of, 97, 98–100
  verbal commons, 96–97
LaRussa Italian foods, 41
Lazzeri, Tony, 126
Leconte, Henri, 21
Led Zeppelin, 140
Lee, Bruce, 70
Lennon, John, 2, 132
Leonardo da Vinci, 82–83, 139
Lessing, Doris, 89
Letterman, David, 132
Letter to D'Alembert (Rousseau), 68

Let Us Now Praise Famous Men (Agee and Evans), 71–72
Lewinsky, Monica, 50, 54, 60
Lewis, Carl, 110, 119
Lichtenstein, Roy, 9, 81
Lincoln, Abraham, 47, 49, 50
Lindbergh, Charles, 19
Liston, Sonny, 119
Lives (Plutarch), 121
Lives (Vasari), 81
Locke, John, 67
Logie Award, 115
Long-term fame vs. short-term fame. *See* Time/temporal aspects of fame
Lost World (film), 106
Louganis, Greg, 22
Louis, Joe, 21, 117, 118
Louvre, 82–83
Lowe, Rob, 48
Luhrmann, Baz, 85
Lycidas (Milton), 156

Madame Tussaud's Wax Museum, 43, 131
Madonna, 5, 24, 25, 63, 163
Mailer, Norman, 84
Maloney, Michael, 152
Maltin, Leonard, 97
Mandeville, Bernard, 11, 146
Manilow, Barry, 6–7
Maradona, Diego, 116
Marcellinus, Ammianus, 128
Marino, Dan, 41
Maris, Roger, 118, 119

Market economy and capitalism, 8, 9, 11–12, 66, 80, 99,
   167–168
   convergence of quality and,
      109–112
   decentralization of, 101
Markets, fame, 8, 9, 10–11, 77, 83
   celebrity endorsements and,
      41–42
   centralization of, 106–107
   competitive, 103–104, 111–112,
      113, 115, 121, 124, 127–129,
      144
   complementary vs. rivalrous,
      119–127, 129
   creativity and, 133–140
   cycles of fame and, 78–81
   delayed entry and reinstate-
      ment into, 82, 84–85, 141
   diversity and decentralization
      of, 103, 104–106, 107, 108,
      109–112
   fame production and,
      114–116, 126
   government policy and,
      164–166
   imperfections in, 164
   inequality in, 107–108
   intermediaries in, 123, 125,
      132
   investment in, 25, 27–28,
      28–29, 113, 128, 142
   packaging of fame, 124–125,
      127, 129
   performance measurement in,
      127–129, 142–143
   privatized, 99–100

publicity in, 25–36
reputation and, 62–63, 77, 141
role of statistics in, 116–117
snowball effects of, 14–16
standards of evaluation,
   61–62, 85
superstar status, 101–112, 113,
   141
supply of fame and, 113–114,
   120, 128–129
trickle-down economics of,
   108–109
winner-take-all, 102
zero-sum nature of, 108,
   113–114, 119, 130, 170
See also Endorsements,
   celebrity; Praise for sale
Marley, Bob, 20
Marsh, David, 34
Marx, Karl, 39
Masaccio (Tomaso Guidi), 81
Masolino da Panicale, 81
Mass culture, 16–22, 40
"Matthew effect" of citation
   practices, 87–92
"Maybellene" (song), 27
McEnroe, John, 118, 124
McGwire, Mark, 110, 118, 119
McKenzie, George, 161
McLuhan, Marshall, 40
McSmith, Andy, 25
Medals. See Prizes and awards
Media, 131. See also
   Publicity/promotion
Melville, Herman, 71
Mementos, 43
Menander, 66

Role models and heroes, 46–47, 63–64, 121
  changing nature of fame and, 47–54
  fame vs. shame and, 54–70
  female, 67–68
  fraudulent, 65–66
  standards for, 67, 68, 69
  violence and, 66–67, 69–70
Rolex watches, 44
Rolling Stone magazine, 34, 92
Rolling Stones, 22, 81, 153, 168. *See also* Jagger, Mick
Romeo and Juliet (Shakespeare), 85
Roosevelt, Franklin Delano, 48, 50, 169
Roosevelt, Theodore, 50
Rosen, Sherwin, 101
Ross, Betsy, 165
Rousseau, Jean-Jacques, 68
Royalty, 1, 5, 52–53. *See also* Diana, Princess
Rubens, Peter Paul, 82–83
Rumors (album by Fleetwood Mac), 103
Ruth, Babe, 48, 83, 109, 111, 112, 116, 118, 126
Rutherford, Ernest, 122

Safire, William, 98
Sainthood, 93–94, 95
Salinger, J. D., 132
Saturday Night Fever (film), 68
Saturday Night Fever (soundtrack), 103
Schelling Thomas, 17

Schmeling, Max, 21
Schopenhauer, Arthur, 71, 88, 150
Schwab, Charles, 22
Schwarzenegger, Arnold, 18, 24, 48, 70
Seinfeld, Jerry, 60, 65
Seinfeld (television show), 105
Selena, 20, 132
Seles, Monica, 132–133
Seurat, Georges, 21
Sex Pistols, 33
Sgt. Pepper (album by the Beatles), 138
Shakespeare, William, 35, 77, 81, 85, 88, 90, 145, 150–151, 156–157
Shame as an aspect of fame, 54–70, 171
Shocker, Urban, 126
Short-term fame vs. long-term fame. *See* Time/temporal aspects of fame
Signaling. *See* Publicity/promotion
Silkwood, Karen, 20
Simmons, Al, 126
Simpson, O. J., 7
Siskel, Gene, 76
Smith, Adam, 2, 111, 152–153, 157, 163, 167
Snoop Doggy Dogg, 104
Social aspects of fame, 2, 8, 9, 11, 12, 15, 57, 64–65, 164, 165, 171
Socrates, 10, 13
Sophists, 10, 12, 167
Sosa, Sammy, 110, 118, 119